50 Walks for
BIRDWATCHERS

Produced by AA Publishing

Introduction and bird information written by Dr Paul Sterry

© Automobile Association Developments Limited 2005
Illustrations © Automobile Association Developments Limited 2005

Published by AA Publishing (a trading name of Automobile Association Developments
Limited, whose registered office is Fanum House, Basing View, Basingstoke, Hampshire RG21
4EA; registered number 1878835)

oS Ordnance Survey® This product includes mapping data licensed from Ordnance Survey® with
the permission of the Controller of Her Majesty's Stationery Office.© Crown
copyright 2005. All rights reserved. Licence number 399221

ISBN-10: 0-7495-4811-8
ISBN-13: 978-0-7495-4811-7

A02780

A CIP catalogue record for this book is available from the British Library.

The contents of this book are believed correct at the time of printing. Nevertheless, the
publishers cannot be held responsible for any errors or omissions or for changes in the
details given in this book or for the consequences of any reliance on the information it
provides. We have tried to ensure accuracy in this book, but things do change and we would
be grateful if readers would advise us of any inaccuracies they may encounter. This does not
affect your statutory rights.

We have taken all reasonable steps to ensure that these walks are safe and achievable by
walkers with a realistic level of fitness. However, all outdoor activities involve a degree of risk
and the publishers accept no responsibility for any injuries caused to readers whilst following
these walks. For more advice on walking safely see page 128.

Visit AA Publishing's website at www.theAA.com/bookshop

Colour reproduction by MRM Graphics Ltd
Printed in Slovenia by MKT PRINT d.d.

Legend

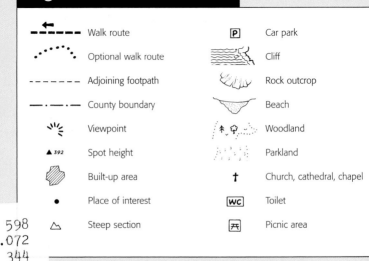

◄– – – – – –	Walk route	℗	Car park
·.·.·.·.·.	Optional walk route	≈≈≈	Cliff
– – – – – –	Adjoining footpath		Rock outcrop
— · — · — · —	County boundary		Beach
☼	Viewpoint	♠ ♣	Woodland
▲ 392	Spot height		Parkland
	Built-up area	†	Church, cathedral, chapel
●	Place of interest	WC	Toilet
△	Steep section	⊼	Picnic area

locator map

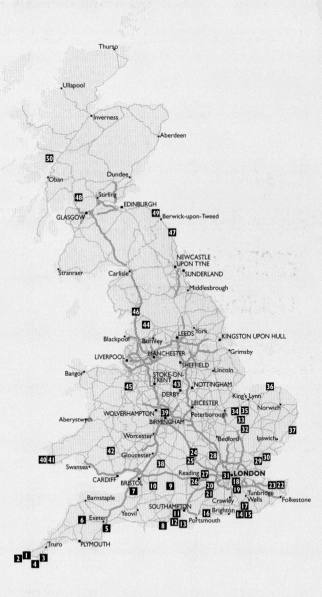

Contents
=======

Contents

WALK		RATING	DISTANCE	PAGE
1	Golden Beaches of Porthcurno	🚶 🚶 🚶	3½ miles (5.7km)	8
2	Gwennap Head and Porthgwarra Cove	🚶 🚶 🚶	2 miles (3.2km)	11
3	Hidden Creeks of Helford	🚶 🚶 🚶	5 miles (8km)	12
4	Wildflower Haven at Mullion	🚶 🚶 🚶	7 miles (11.3km)	15
5	Exeter to Topsham Canal	🚶 🚶 🚶	4 miles (6.4km)	18
6	Along the Tarka Trail in Devon	🚶 🚶 🚶	7 miles (11.3km)	20
7	Westhay Peatland Reserve	🚶 🚶 🚶	4¾ miles (7.7km)	22
8	Studland's Sand and Heath	🚶 🚶 🚶	7 miles (11.3km)	25
9	Vale of Pewsey and Oare Hill	🚶 🚶 🚶	5 miles (8km)	28
10	Westbury White Horse	🚶 🚶 🚶	4 miles (6.4km)	30
11	New Forest Trails	🚶 🚶 🚶	6 miles (9.7km)	32
12	Rhinefield Ornamental Drive	🚶 🚶 🚶	2 miles (3.2km)	35
13	Newtown and its Estuary	🚶 🚶 🚶	3½ miles (5.7km)	36
14	Snake River and the Seven Sisters	🚶 🚶 🚶	3 miles (4.8km)	38
15	Cuckmere River and Charleston Manor	🚶 🚶 🚶	5¾ miles (9.3km)	41
16	Views and Yews at Kingley Vale	🚶 🚶 🚶	5 miles (8km)	42
17	Arlington's Lakeside Trail	🚶 🚶	3 miles (4.8km)	45
18	Happy Valley and Chaldon's Lucky Escape	🚶 🚶 🚶	3 miles (5km)	48
19	A North Downs Loops at Chaldon	🚶 🚶 🚶	5½ miles (9km)	51
20	A Pilgrimage to Waverley	🚶 🚶 🚶	3 miles (4.8km)	52
21	A Frensham Loop	🚶 🚶 🚶	3 miles (4.8km)	55
22	A Circuit at Stodmarsh	🚶 🚶 🚶	4 miles (6.4km)	56
23	Blean's Ancient Woodlands	🚶 🚶 🚶	5 miles (8km)	58
24	Bewitched Otmoor–the Forgotten Land	🚶 🚶 🚶	4 miles (6.4km)	60
25	Noke-at the Trees	🚶 🚶 🚶	8 miles (12.9km)	63
26	Enduring Brimpton	🚶 🚶 🚶	6 miles (9.7km)	64
27	Dinton Pastures	🚶 🚶 🚶	3 miles (4.8km)	67
28	The Canal Reservoirs	🚶 🚶 🚶	4½ miles (7.2km)	70
29	Danbury Country Park	🚶 🚶 🚶	4 miles (6.4km)	72

Contents

WALK	RATING	DISTANCE	PAGE
30 Danbury Wildlife	🚶🚶🚶	5½ miles (8.8km)	75
31 The Wetland Birds of Barnes	🚶🚶🚶	3¾ miles (6km)	76
32 Wicken–the Last Survivor	🚶🚶🚶	4¾ miles (7.7km)	79
33 Fenland's Big Skies	🚶🚶🚶	6¼ miles (10.1km)	82
34 Twitching in Ouse Washes	🚶🚶🚶	10 miles (16.1km)	85
35 Welney's Birds	🚶🚶🚶	4¼ miles (6.8km)	86
36 Blakeney Eye's Magical Marshes	🚶🚶🚶	4½ miles (7.2km)	88
37 The Ghosts of Dunwich	🚶🚶🚶	8 miles (12.9km)	91
38 Cotswold Water Park	🚶🚶🚶	5 miles (8km)	94
39 Sandwell Valley Park	🚶🚶🚶	4 miles (6.4km)	97
40 Marloes Peninsula	🚶🚶🚶	6 miles (9.7km)	100
41 St Brides Haven and the Marloes Peninsula	🚶🚶🚶	10 miles (16.1km)	103
42 Pen y Fan–a Circular Route	🚶🚶🚶	5 miles (8km)	104
43 Around Carsington Reservoir	🚶🚶🚶	8 miles (12.9km)	106
44 Gisburn Forest	🚶🚶🚶	3 miles (4.8km)	108
45 Meres, Mosses and Moraines at Ellesmere	🚶🚶🚶	7¼ miles (11.7km)	111
46 High Arnside Knott	🚶🚶🚶	5½ miles (8.8km)	114
47 Bamburgh's Coast and Castle	🚶🚶🚶	8½ miles (13.7km)	116
48 A Trail Through the Sallochy Woods	🚶🚶🚶	2 miles (3.2km)	119
49 A Windy Walk to St Abb's Head	🚶🚶🚶	4 miles (6.4km)	122
50 Ariundle Oakwoods	🚶🚶🚶	7 miles (11.3km)	125

Rating: Each walk is rated for its relative difficulty compared to the other walks in this book. Walks marked 🚶🚶🚶 are likely to be shorter and easier with little total ascent. The hardest walks are marked 🚶🚶🚶 .

Walking in Safety: For advice and safety tips ➤ 128.

Introduction

Birdwatching has never been more popular than it is today. Millions of people are members of bird-related conservation organisations and even more enjoy observing them on a casual basis. In part, our interest in birds stems from their relative abundance in the countryside and the ease with which they can be seen, often at relatively close quarters. But the inherent elegance and beauty of birds is also an undeniable factor.

Birds are fascinating to observe and sometimes a challenge to identify. Their ability to fly and their consequent apparent freedom has always appealed to and intrigued us. But in recent times they have also come to symbolise all that is vulnerable and precious in our environment: like other forms of wildlife almost all bird species are adversely affected by the way that we, as a society, live our lives and the plight of birds is indicative of our impact on the environment. Consequently, most people get a real thrill from seeing birds in good numbers and for many the sight of a soaring buzzard, or a flock of lapwings, is an almost life-affirming indication that there are still many positive aspects to the British countryside.

For many people birdwatching goes hand-in-hand with walking in the countryside. Hardly surprising, since most species favour rural habitats and landscapes where the backdrop is one of natural beauty. *50 Walks for Birdwatchers* aims to combine these two pleasurable pastimes. Over the last 20 years, AA Publishing has produced countless guided walks covering most parts of the British countryside. Recognising the links between walking in the countryside and an interest in birds, we have also published a number of definitive titles on birds such as the *Illustrated Guide to the Birds of Britain and Europe*.

Britain has such a wealth of birdwatching locations that it is always going to be difficult to choose just 50 walks. More experienced birdwatchers among you will notice the absence of a number of prime birdwatching locations from this book. Very popular, well-known sites such as Minsmere RSPB reserve in Suffolk and Slimbridge WWT reserve in Gloucestershire can be overcrowded and their best opportunities rely mainly on observations from hides.

The routes chosen for this book combine excellent birdwatching with a good walk in the countryside and a sense of peace and quiet. We have been mindful of the need to produce an even geographical spread across the region. Perceptive readers among you will notice that a significant proportion of the routes pass alongside water for at least part of their duration. This is not just coincidence. Coastal and fresh water acts like a magnet for birds (as well as walkers) and by including watery locations in the walks the aim is to increase greatly the number and variety of birds with which you come into contact. So we hope you enjoy these walks in the British countryside and discover some of the region's wonderful birdlife at the same time.

Using this Book

Information panels

An information panel for each walk shows its relative difficulty, the distance and total amount of ascent. An indication of the gradients you will encounter is shown by the rating ▲ ▲ ▲ (no steep slopes) to ▲ ▲ ▲ (several very steep slopes).

Maps

Some walks have a suggested option in the same area. The information panel for these walks will tell you how much extra walking is involved. Where an option returns to the same point on the main walk, just the distance of the loop is given. Where an option leaves the main walk at one point and returns to it at another, then the distance shown is for the whole walk. The minimum time suggested is for reasonably fit walkers and doesn't allow for stops. Each walk has a suggested OS map which we always recommend that you take with you. Laminated aqua3 maps are long lasting and are water resistant.

Start Points

The start of each walk is given as a six-figure grid reference prefixed by two letters indicating which 100km square of the National Grid it refers to. You'll find more information on grid references on most Ordnance Survey maps.

Dogs

We have tried to give dog owners useful advice about how dog friendly each walk is. Please respect other countryside users. Keep your dog under control, especially around livestock, and obey local bylaws and other dog control notices.

Car Parking

Many of the car parks suggested are public, but occasionally you may find you have to park on the roadside or in a lay-by. Please be considerate when you leave your car, ensuring that access roads or gates are not blocked and that other vehicles can pass safely. Remember that pub car parks are private and should not be used unless you have the owner's permission.

Golden Beaches and Cliffs at Porthcurno

Along interlocking footpaths between sandy coves and granite cliffs on the Land's End Peninsula.

•DISTANCE•	3½ miles (5.7km)
•MINIMUM TIME•	2hrs 30min
•ASCENT / GRADIENT•	164ft (50m) ▲▲▲
•LEVEL OF DIFFICULTY•	🚶🚶 🚶🚶
•PATHS•	Coastal footpath
•LANDSCAPE•	Granite sea cliffs and inland heath
•SUGGESTED MAP•	aqua3 OS Explorer 107 St Austell & Liskeard
•START / FINISH•	Grid reference: SW 384224
•DOG FRIENDLINESS•	Dogs should be kept under control on beaches
•PARKING•	Porthcurno, St Levan and Porthgwarra
•PUBLIC TOILETS•	Porthgwarra and Porthleven

BACKGROUND TO THE WALK

Land's End may be the ultimate visitor destination in Cornwall. It is the most westerly point certainly and its cliffs are nothing less than spectacular; but for the true aficionado of coastal scenery, the granite cliffs of Porthcurno and Porthgwarra, to the south of Land's End, are hard to beat for their beauty and sculpted form. The area has even more esoteric distinction. Gwennap Head, at Porthgwarra, is the most southerly point on the Land's End Peninsula. The Atlantic tidal flow divides at the base of Gwennap's spectacular Chair Ladder cliff, one flow running eastwards up the English Channel, the other running north, up St George's Channel between Britain and Ireland. Partly because of this, Gwennap Head is sometimes known as 'the Fishermen's Land's End', a title that rather puts the other Land's End in its place.

Golden Sand

This walk starts at Porthcurno, where a sweeping expanse of almost white shell sand lies at the heart of an arc of golden granite cliffs that embrace the small bay. On the south side lies the rocky coxcomb of Treryn Dinas, or Logan Rock. To the north is the famous Minack Open Air Theatre, built within the rocky ribs of the headland. The final section of the walk passes the Minack, but first the route leads inland and across fields to the splendid little Church of St Levan, couched in one of the few sheltered spots on this robust coast. Below the church a shallow valley runs down to Chapel Porth Beach, more besieged by tides than Porthcurno, but still a delightful place, especially in summer. Again the beach here is left for later in the walk, whose route now leads along the coast path and then climbs inland before dropping down to Porthgwarra Cove, where tunnels and caverns in the cliff were carved out by farmers and fishermen to give better access to the narrow beach. From Porthgwarra, you head back along the coast path to Porth Chapel. The path leads you down past the little Well of St Levan. Below here there is a rocky access path to the beach.

Spectacular Steps

The route of the walk leads steeply up to Rospletha Point and then to the remarkable cliff face theatre at Minack (➤ What to Look For). From here, the most direct way down to Porthcurno Beach is by a series of very steep steps that may not suit everyone. But if you don't mind the vertiginous experience, the views really are outstanding. You can avoid this descent by some judicious road walking. Either way Porthcurno's glorious beach is at hand in the cove below you.

Walk 1

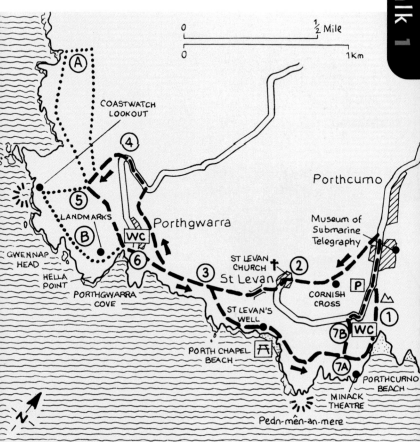

Walk 1 Directions

① From the car park, walk back up the approach road, then just beyond the **Porthcurno Hotel**, turn sharply left along a track and follow it to reach cottages. Pass to the right of the cottages and go through a metal kissing gate. Follow a field path past a granite cross.

② Enter **St Levan** churchyard by a granite stile. Go round the far side of the church to the entrance gate and onto a surfaced lane. Cross the lane and follow the path opposite, signposted '**Porthgwarra Cove**'. Cross a footbridge over a stream then in about 55yds (50m), at a junction, take the right fork and follow the path to merge with the main coast path and keep ahead.

③ Just after the path begins to descend towards **Porthgwarra Cove**, branch off right up some wooden steps. Reach a track and turn up right, then at a road, turn left.

④ Go round a sharp left-hand bend, then at a footpath signpost, go right down a grassy path and cross a stone footbridge. Continue uphill to reach a bend on a track, just up from large granite houses.

⑤ Turn left, go over a stile beside a gate, then continue down a surfaced lane to **Porthgwarra Cove**.

WHERE TO EAT AND DRINK

There is a seasonal café at **Porthgwarra**, ideally located at the midway point in the walk. Porthcurno has several outlets including the **Beach Café** and the **Cable Inn**. A seasonal ice cream and soft drinks van is usually located in the Porthcurno car park.

Opposite the shop and café, go right down a track, signposted '**Coast Path**' then follow the path round left in front of a house. Go sharp right at a junction and climb steps.

⑥ Continue along the coast path, partly reversing the previous route past Point ④. Keep right at junctions, and eventually descend

---

FOR BIRDWATCHERS

Renowned as a migration hotspot, the area is the first landfall in spring for birds arriving from Europe, while in autumn species gather here before heading out to sea on their return journey. Swallow, chiffchaff and whitethroat are regularly encountered and there is always a chance of finding something more unusual. Wryneck and ortolan bunting can be seen every year.

---

past **St Levan's Well** to just above **Porth Chapel Beach**. (Dogs should be kept under control on the beach.) Follow the coast path steeply over **Pedn-mên-an-mere**, and continue to the car park of the **Minack Theatre**.

⑦ For the surefooted, cross the car park and go down the track to the left of the **Minack** compound, then descend the steep and dramatic cliff steps, with great care. When the path levels off, continue to a junction. The right fork takes you to **Porthcurno Beach** and back to the car park. The continuation leads to the road opposite the **Beach Café**, where a right turn leads to the car park. A less challenging alternative to the cliff steps is to turn left out of the Minack car park. Follow the approach road to a T-junction with a public road. Turn right and walk down the road, watching out for traffic.

WHAT TO LOOK FOR

The **Minack Theatre** was the unusual creation of Rowena Cade, whose family bought the rocky headland above Porthcurno Beach in the 1920s. A general interest in theatre led to the staging of Shakespeare's *The Tempest* on a makeshift stage on the cliffs in 1932. Miss Cade, ably assisted by skilled local gardeners and builders then developed the Minack over many years into a full scale theatre, carved out of the cliffs, a Cornish version in miniature of the great classical theatres of Greece and Rome, but with a stupendous backdrop. Today atmospheric performances of a variety of plays and musicals are staged during the summer months. A Minack performance is an unbeatable experience. Wine and light clothes for balmy summer evenings; full scale waterproofs and hot chocolate otherwise.

Gwennap Head and Porthgwarra Cove

A short extension to Walk 1 takes you across 'the Fishermen's Land's End'.
See map and information panel for Walk 1

•DISTANCE•	2 miles (3.2km) for this extra loop
•MINIMUM TIME•	1hr
•ASCENT / GRADIENT•	164ft (50m) ▲ ▲ ▲
•LEVEL OF DIFFICULTY•	👫 👫 👫

Walk 2 Directions
(See map for Walk 1)

You can extend the main walk by following the coast path across **Gwennap Head** to the west of **Porthgwarra Cove**. At Point ⑤ on the main walk turn right onto the rough track, then, at the left-hand bend, go off right along a grassy track. In 30yds (27m), where the track forks, take the right fork and follow a grassy track across the open heathland, a glorious mosaic of purple heather and golden gorse in late summer. Keep left at the next fork and soon pass through a gap in a lichened granite wall. A few paces beyond the wall, take the left fork at a junction of tracks. Keep ahead along the track to reach the coast path, Point Ⓐ, by an old tyre capstan, once used as part of a moving target line for military rifle training. Turn left here along a short path and in a few steps merge with the main coast path abreast of a big lichen-covered rock.

Go through the granite wall ahead and at a fork keep left and descend gently to the bend in the track by Point ⑤ once more. Turn right up the track, then, in about 30yds (27m), turn off right up a narrow path that leads to the **National Coastwatch lookout**, where you turn left along the coast path. Follow the path past two incongruous, brightly painted concrete cones, Point Ⓑ, protruding from the heather. These are not Cornish missiles that failed to make it out of their silos. They are landmarks to assist mariners in fixing the position of the dangerous **Runnelstone Reef**, also marked offshore by a buoy whose wind-activated siren can often be heard moaning eerily. Follow the coast path all the way round **Hella Point** to reach the surfaced road above **Porthgwarra Cove** where you re-join Walk 48 at Point ⑤.

FOR BIRDWATCHERS

Seabirds, notably gannets and manx shearwaters, can be seen from most headlands on the Land's End peninsula, often in large numbers during the summer months. But the prospect of finding a Cory's or sooty shearwater is this particular stretch of coastline's big attraction for sea-watching enthusiasts and Porthgwarra is generally reckoned to be the best spot for this pursuit.¶

Hidden Creeks of Helford

A circuit of some of the peaceful tidal creeks of the Helford Estuary.

•DISTANCE•	5 miles (8km)
•MINIMUM TIME•	3hrs
•ASCENT / GRADIENT•	328ft (100m) ▲ ▲ ▲
•LEVEL OF DIFFICULTY•	🚶🚶 🚶🚶 🚶
•PATHS•	Good woodland paths and tracks and field paths. Short section of quiet lane, 10 stiles
•LANDSCAPE•	Wooded creekside and fields
•SUGGESTED MAP•	aqua3 OS Explorer 103 The Lizard
•START / FINISH•	Grid reference: SW 759261
•DOG FRIENDLINESS•	Dogs must be kept under strict control between Treath and St Anthony
•PARKING•	Helford car park. Large car park overlooking creek. Can become busy in summer. Only authorised cars are allowed beyond the car park into the village of Helford
•PUBLIC TOILETS•	Helford car park

BACKGROUND TO THE WALK

The Helford River is enduringly popular with land-based visitors and leisure sailors alike, yet the area manages somehow to absorb it all. Cars probe tentatively between the unforgiving stone hedges of narrow Cornish lanes. The bulk of river craft are yachts, so that on a busy sailing day you will hear only the pleasing flap of sails blowing through, as flocks of vessels tack across the estuary mouth. The pelt of trees that lines the estuary and its subsidiary creeks plays a great part in this muffling of too much human racket.

Picturesque
Yet the picturesque, leisure-dominated Helford of today was once a bustling haven for all sorts of trade, and not least, was a haven for pirates and smugglers. During Elizabethan times especially, a passel of Cornish rascals, from the highest in the land to the lowest, was engaged in plundering the cargoes of vessels that sailed through the Channel approaches. The Helford, as it is popularly known, was a secretive, useful base from which all manner of goods could be spirited away inland. In later times the river became an equally secretive base for missions against German-occupied France during the Second World War.

There is little physical evidence of any of this busy past, but in the shrouded creeks that run off like fibrous roots from the main river it is easy to imagine the utter remoteness of life hundreds of years ago, when movement by sea was far more convenient than by land. This walk starts from the village of Helford and follows the southern shore of the estuary between Treath and Dennis Head, mainly through the deep woodland of the Bosahan estate. There are tantalising glimpses of the river through the trees and the path skirts tiny coves such as Bosahan and Ponsence with their inviting beaches that must surely have seen their share of night-landings in the piratical past.

The return leg of the walk follows the north shore of the adjacent Gillan Creek, far smaller and thus far less accommodating to vessels than the deep Helford. Here the tiny

½ Mile

1 Km

Frenchman's Pill

Frenchman's Creek

Kestle

PENARVON COVE

Helford

⑦

SHIPWRIGHT'S ARMS

①　P

Helford Point

Helford Passage

⑥

CHURCH OF ST MANACCA

THE NEW INN

⑤

Treath

Manaccan

ROSCADDON

Bosahan

Helford River

④

Carne

Bosahan Cove

St Anthony-in-Meneage

Gillan Creek

Ponsence Cove

Flushing

②

Gillan

St Anthony Church

Gillan Harbour

③

NAVIGATION MARKS

Toll Point

Optional circuit of Dennis Head

DENNIS HEAD

-N→

Church of St Anthony adds to the overall serenity. From near the head of the creek, you climb inland to Manaccan, a charming hamlet that seems to tumble down the slopes of the valley. Beyond the village the route leads into the wooded valley above Helford and takes you back to your starting point through chequered shade.

Walk 3 Directions

① As you leave the car park, turn left along a path, signed '**Coast Path**'. Go through a metal gate and follow a sunken track. Descend steps, then turn right along a lane. At a steep right-hand bend, bear off ahead along a track. Follow this permissive path through trees, keeping left at any junctions.

② Leave the wooded area via a metal gate, then turn left along a field edge to a stone stile, Follow the bottom edge of the next two fields. Cross a fence at a field gap beside a white pole and a red post and triangle (these are navigation marks). Follow the field edge ahead. Go through a kissing gate, then follow the field edge (there's a seat and viewpoint on the left), to where it ends at the beginning of a wide track (to make the short circuit of **Dennis Head**, follow the track ahead to a stile on the left).

③ To continue on the main route, turn sharply right at the start of the wide track and follow the left-hand field edge and then a path across the open field. Join a track behind a house, then go through a kissing gate and descend to **St Anthony's Church**. Follow the road alongside **Gillan Creek**.

④ Just past where the road curves round a bay, go up right between granite gate posts by a public footpath sign. Follow a broad track through trees to houses at **Roscadden**. Keep ahead along a track that leads to **Manaccan** at a T-junction opposite **Manaccan Church**.

⑤ Go through the churchyard and on through the gate opposite to a road (the village shop is to the left). Keep ahead to a junction, the New Inn is down to the left, then go up right, past the school. Keep uphill, then turn left along **Minster Meadow**, go over a stile, and through two fields to reach a road.

⑥ Go diagonally left to the stile opposite, cross a field, then go left following signposts to reach woods. Follow the path ahead. At a junction keep ahead, go over a stile and reach a second junction. The extended walk starts here.

⑦ Bear down right and follow a broad track through trees to reach some buildings at **Helford**. Keep ahead on reaching a surfaced road and follow the road uphill to the **car park**.

FOR BIRDWATCHERS

The Helford's tidal creeks support a rich variety of marine life, which in turn feeds large numbers of birds. Redshank, curlew and other waders are most numerous from autumn to spring but gleaming white little egrets are present throughout the year. Keep an eye on the skies too for passing common buzzards and ravens.

Wildflower Haven at Mullion

The heathland of the Lizard Peninsula supports some of the most remarkable of Britain's wild flowers.

•DISTANCE•	7 miles (11.3km)
•MINIMUM TIME•	4hrs
•ASCENT / GRADIENT•	164ft (50m) ▲ ▲ ▲
•LEVEL OF DIFFICULTY•	🚶 🚶 🚶
•PATHS•	Good inland tracks and paths, can be muddy in places during wet weather. Coastal footpath, 21 stiles
•LANDSCAPE•	Flat heathland and high sea cliff
•SUGGESTED MAP•	aqua3 OS Explorer 103 The Lizard
•START / FINISH•	Grid reference: SW 669162
•DOG FRIENDLINESS•	Dogs on lead through grazed areas. Notices indicate
•PARKING•	Predannack Wollas Farm car park (National Trust)
•PUBLIC TOILETS•	Mullion Cove, 200yds (183m) up road from harbour

BACKGROUND TO THE WALK

The heathland of the Lizard Peninsula near Mullion lacks the rugged beauty of Cornwall's granite moors; its flatness seems a dull contrast to the dramatic sea cliffs that define its edges; the only punctuation marks are the huge satellite dishes of the nearby Goonhilly tracking station and the lazily revolving blades of modern wind turbines. Yet, beneath the skin, this seemingly featureless landscape is botanically unique and exciting, not least because the Lizard's calcareous soil is rich in magnesium and supports plants that are more often seen in chalk or limestone regions. The warming influence of the sea and the area's generally mild and frost-free climate encourages growth.

Famous Plant
The Lizard's most famous plant is the Cornish heath, rare in Britain generally, but abundant on the Lizard. In full bloom it contributes to a glorious mosaic of colour, its pink and white flowers matched by the brilliant yellow of Western gorse and the deeper pinks of cross-leaved heath and bell heather. From the very start of the walk you are at the heart of the heathland. More common plants include spring squill, thrift and foxglove. Deeper into the heath are a variety of orchids including the rare green winged orchid, with its purple-lipped flowers.

Soapy Cove
Near the turning point of the walk you pass close to the old wartime Predannack airfield from where modern gliders soar into the air. Soon, the route joins the coast at Gew Graze, a feature that is also known as 'Soapy Cove' because of the presence of steatite, or soapstone. This is a fairly rare type of rock which was once used in the 18th-century production of china and porcelain. The final part of the route, along the cliffs to Mullion Cove, brings more flower spotting opportunities. On the path out of Gew Graze look for the yellow bracts and

purple florets of carline thistle; the straw-coloured bracts curl over the flowerheads to protect them in wet weather.

Another remarkable plant is thyme broomrape, a dark reddish-brown, almost dead-looking plant that obtains its chlorophyll as a parasite growing on thyme. Such plants are often difficult to spot, whereas the smooth grassy slopes of the cliff tops near Mullion are a riot of powder blue spring squill, white sea campion and the yellow heads of lesser celandine and kidney vetch.

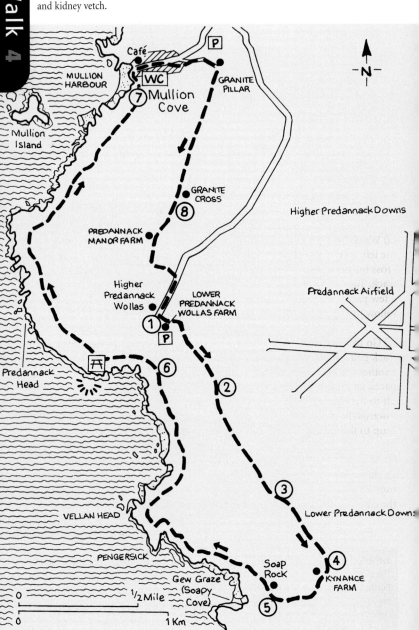

Walk 4 Directions

FOR BIRDWATCHERS
Set against a stunning floral backdrop, look for species such as stonechat, whitethroat and the occasional Dartford warbler as you pass by swathes of gorse. Along the coast, keep an eye open for unusual seabirds such as shearwaters if onshore winds prevail; There is even a chance of seeing a chough – the species has returned to the Lizard in the last few years after an absence of several decades.

① Leave **Predannack Wollas Farm** car park by its bottom end. Follow the winding track ahead for just under ½ mile (800m) to where it ends at a gate. (Ignore a signposted track going off left just before this gate.) Beyond the gate, bear left to a stile. Follow the edge of the next field to a stile, then continue to open ground by a gate in a fence on the right.

② Go over the stile next to the gate, then bear away at an angle from the fence along a path to reach English Nature's **Kynance Farm Nature Reserve**. Keep ahead towards distant buildings.

③ Watch for a gap in the hedge on the left, go through the gap, then cross the next field to reach a rough track. Turn right along the track for a few paces then bear off left and follow the edge of the scrub.

④ Go through a gate, then follow a track going right. Merge with another track, and then in a few paces, and just before a ford, bear off to the right along a track towards the coast (**Kynance Farm** is up to the right).

⑤ At a crossing with the coast path, go right and steeply uphill, then go over a stile onto the cliff top. Follow the coast path as it winds round the edge of the often projecting cliffs at **Pengersick** and **Vellan Head**.

⑥ Go left at a junction, just past a National Trust sign for '**Predannack**'. (You can return to the car park by following the inland path from here.) Cross a stream in a dip and climb up left and continue along the coast path to **Mullion Cove** and Harbour.

⑦ Go up the road from **Mullion Harbour** and just beyond the public toilets and the shop, turn off right at a coast path sign. Keep to the right of the entrance to a holiday residential site and follow a track uphill. On a bend and just before a granite pillar, go off right and over a stone stile. Follow the path ahead through a grove of thorn trees and then through fields.

⑧ Pass a tall granite cross and then reach a lane and turn right along the lane towards the farm. Just before **Predannack Manor Farm** entrance, go left over a stile by a field gate, then turn right along the field edge. Go over a stile, then left along a hedged-in path, cross a stile and cross two fields to reach a lane (watch for traffic). Turn right to **Predannack Wollas Farm** car park.

WHERE TO EAT AND DRINK ⓘ
There is a café at Mullion Harbour, the **Porthmellin Café**, serving full cooked breakfast, morning coffee, cream teas, crab sandwiches, ice creams and soft drinks. Open Easter to September.

Walk 5

The Historic Exeter to Topsham Canal

A stroll along the very first English canal to use locks – and a look at the old port of Topsham.

•DISTANCE•	4 miles (6.4km)
•MINIMUM TIME•	2hrs
•ASCENT / GRADIENT•	Negligible
•LEVEL OF DIFFICULTY•	
•PATHS•	Level tow paths
•LANDSCAPE•	River estuary; extensive mudflats at low tide
•SUGGESTED MAP•	aqua3 OS Explorer 110 Torquay & Dawlish
•START / FINISH•	Grid reference: SX 972844
•DOG FRIENDLINESS•	Watch out for wildlife – and mountain bikes
•PARKING•	By St Clement's Church, Powderham
•PUBLIC TOILETS•	Turf Hotel, Passage House Inn, by fire station in Topsham

Walk 5 Directions

This easy walk along the picturesque estuary of the River Exe has a huge amount to offer. You can visit medieval **Powderham Castle**, which is open to visitors from April to October (excluding Saturdays) and you can see the oldest ship canal in the country. There are usually boat trips to watch the rare avocets here in February – and a ferry ride takes you to the historic port of **Topsham**.

St Clement's Church, where you leave your car, is situated on the very edge of the **Powderham Estate**, the historic family home of the Earls of Devon. The original building dates back to the late 14th century when it was the home of Sir Philip Courtenay. Extensive damage caused during the Civil War was followed by a comprehensive programme of restoration in the 18th and 19th centuries.

The walk starts down the lane past the church towards the river. After a few paces turn left to join the **South West Way** (unmarked as such) which follows the **Exeter-to-Penzance railway** line here, running along the bank of the Exe estuary. Walk along the path to cross the railway. Turn left to walk upriver; there are superb views to (from left to right) Topsham, Exton, the Royal Marine Commandos Training Centre, Lympstone and Exmouth. Within 20 minutes you should reach the outlet of the

FOR BIRDWATCHERS

The upper reaches of the Exe estuary are encountered on this walk. Although there is something to see throughout the year, October to March are the best months and tens of thousands of waders, ducks and geese congregate here. Redshank, dunlin and ringed plover are common and there is a real chance of seeing avocets on this route – a flock of several hundred spends the winter in the area.

Exeter Ship Canal at the **Turf Lock**, with the **Turf Hotel** beyond.

The original canal here – the first English lock canal – was begun in 1563, and ran from Exeter to Matford Brook. It was extended to Topsham in 1676, and then to the Turf, enabling trade vessels of over 300 tons to reach Exeter again (the estuary had silted up during the 14th century). In 1827 the Exeter to Topsham Canal was deepened and extended a further 2 miles (3.2km) to the Turf Lock, giving it a total length of 5¼ miles (8.4km). The building which now houses the Turf Hotel was probably built to accommodate visiting boat crews and their horses. The horses were used to pull the barges up the canal to Exeter.

The original lock gates can be seen beside the canal. Made of wood and weighing 15 tons, these were opened and closed by hand-operated winches, requiring enormous strength; they needed constant repair, and were replaced every 50 years. The gates currently in use are made of steel and are electronically operated.

Don't go over the lock gates here (unless you are in need of refreshment already!) but keep straight on up the canal. This stretch is beautiful, with bulrushes and waterlilies lining the banks, and is popular with canoeists. The only problem with the tow path here is that you are under constant threat from mountain bikers – but you can always catch the *White Heather*

> **WHERE TO EAT AND DRINK** ⓘ
>
> The **Turf Hotel**, in a fantastic position on a narrow point of land where the canal meets the River Exe, is a free house with excellent food – and no chips! Open from the start of April until early November, there are camping facilities here, making the most of its unique setting. The **Passage House Inn** by the ferry in Topsham specialises in seafood and welcomes families. It's a great place to sit outside and watch the goings on up and down the river.

launch for a change of scene (which operates daily from Exeter Quay to the Turf Hotel).

When you reach a small bridge over the canal, cross over to reach the **Topsham ferry slipway**. The ferry runs every day except Tuesday, April to September 11AM–5.30PM and at weekends and bank holidays October to March, but is always dependant on tide and weather. You can hail the ferryman if he's not already waiting for you. Catch the ferry over and have a drink at the **Passage House Inn** and, if you have time, take a look round **Topsham** itself. An important port since Roman times, it prospered greatly when shipping could no longer reach Exeter, and its eventful history has been based largely on shipbuilding and smuggling. Today life in Topsham is somewhat less dramatic. The estuary is used mainly by commercial and pleasure craft, and by thousands of birds who return each year to feed on the mudflats.

Finding your way back to your car from here should be fairly easy.

Along the Tarka Trail in Devon

From the old market town of Hatherleigh to the idyllic village of Iddesleigh.

•DISTANCE•	7 miles (11.3km)
•MINIMUM TIME•	3hrs
•ASCENT / GRADIENT•	245ft (75m) ▲ ▲ ▲
•LEVEL OF DIFFICULTY•	🚶🚶 🚶🚶 🚶🚶
•PATHS•	Fields and country lanes
•LANDSCAPE•	Rolling farmland and wooded valleys
•SUGGESTED MAP•	aqua3 OS Explorer 113 Okehampton
•START / FINISH•	Grid reference: SS 541044
•DOG FRIENDLINESS•	Dogs should be kept under control at all times, livestock in some fields
•PARKING•	Main car park in Hatherleigh
•PUBLIC TOILETS•	In the square, Market Street, Hatherleigh

Walk 6 Directions

The Tarka Trail, attributed to North Devon author Henry Williamson's classic book *Tarka the Otter*, runs for 180 miles (290km) through peaceful countryside, signed, most appropriately, with an otter paw. The trail covers a huge area, from Okehampton on the edge of Dartmoor, across the course of the Taw and Torridge rivers, to Ilfracombe on the coast, and east to Lynton and Exmoor. It forms a large figure-of-eight, following the old Barnstaple-to-Bideford railway line, various rights of way and permissive paths, and provides excellent opportunities for quiet exploration.

This route follows a part of the trail that is only open to walkers, and starts in the market town of **Hatherleigh**, an important centre for North and West Devon. Originally a Saxon settlement, the town developed as a staging post on the main route from Bideford to Exeter, and to Plymouth. A great fire in 1840 destroyed much of the early fabric of the town.

Leave the car park (look out for the wonderful 'Sheep' sculpture) and turn left up **Bridge Street** and then **Market Street**, walking past the square and the parish church (St John the Baptist – now beautifully restored after the mid-15th century

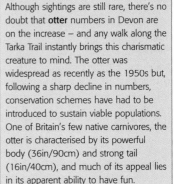

WHAT TO LOOK FOR ⓘ
Although sightings are still rare, there's no doubt that **otter** numbers in Devon are on the increase – and any walk along the Tarka Trail instantly brings this charismatic creature to mind. The otter was widespread as recently as the 1950s but, following a sharp decline in numbers, conservation schemes have had to be introduced to sustain viable populations. One of Britain's few native carnivores, the otter is characterised by its powerful body (36in/90cm) and strong tail (16in/40cm), and much of its appeal lies in its apparent ability to have fun.

Walk 6

54ft (16.5m) spire plunged through the roof of the nave in the storms of January 1990).

At the top of the hill follow the road left, then turn right up **Sanctuary Lane** (signed 'to public footpath'). The lane climbs steeply; ignore all footpath signs until you pass **Wingate** at the hilltop; the lane bends sharp left. Go straight ahead through a gate into a field, signed '**Tarka Trail**'. Walk straight across the field, through two gates, then across the next, keeping left of four big oak trees.

Leave the boggy field through a gate and pass through a coniferous plantation, over a footbridge and kissing gate and into a field. Walk straight over that field, over a stile and through the grounds of **Groves Fishleigh**. Go down the drive and through the gateposts to a T-junction. Turn right towards **Arnold's Fishleigh**. At the edge of the farm buildings turn sharp right (footpath sign) through a gate/stile into a small orchard. Turn left, then out over a stile and plank bridge under big oaks. Turn left and at the end of the field cross the stile, then keep right down the next field. Turn right through a gate/stile, then left through the next gateway, and follow the track downhill to cross the **Okement River** via a cantilevered gate/wooden bridge.

Turn left and walk along the riverbank, then right at the hedge. Go through the next gate, across the corner of the field and through a gate onto a green lane, running uphill. Follow footpath signs right through a gate, and cross the field

FOR BIRDWATCHERS

This walk takes in classic Devon countryside and you are almost guaranteed to see common buzzards and ravens – listen out for the mewing call of the former and the raucous 'cronk' call of the latter. As you pass byz flowing water, watch for dippers and grey wagtails perched on waterside boulders. If you are really lucky you might even see a kingfisher.

to **Nethercott Barton**. Go through the gate, turn left and follow the track uphill (note **Nethercott House** on the left). When the track meets a lane, turn left.

At **Parsonage Gate**, turn right down the drive to **Rectory Farm**, then right at the gates before the farmhouse. Pass through a metal gate to cross the farmyard, then through a gate (marked by an otter paw) and straight ahead. Take the right-hand gate at the end of that field (views left to **Iddesleigh**), and follow the muddy track downhill. Leave the field through a gate onto a green lane. Turn left at the tarmac lane and uphill. Turn right opposite the 15th-century **St James' Church**, then left to the pub.
Note: For a different route home, retrace your steps down the lane from the church, and keep going until **Vellaford Cross**. Turn right along the lane on **Hatherleigh Moor** – the views south to Dartmoor should not be missed. Pass the 1860 **Hatherleigh Monument**, commemorating the distinguished actions of Lt Col William Morris at the Charge of the Light Brigade. Past the Hatherleigh sign, turn right down **Park Road** to reach the top of **Market Street**.

Walk 7

Westhay Peatland Reserve

A nature ramble through reconstructed peat marshland, including a brief walk on water.

•DISTANCE•	4¾ miles (7.7km)
•MINIMUM TIME•	2hrs 15min
•ASCENT / GRADIENT•	250ft (80m) ▲ ▲ ▲
•LEVEL OF DIFFICULTY•	🚶 🚶 🚶
•PATHS•	Mostly smooth, level paths and tracks, 2 stiles
•LANDSCAPE•	Reed beds and water-meadows
•SUGGESTED MAP•	aqua3 OS Explorer 141 Cheddar Gorge
•START / FINISH•	Grid reference: ST 456437
•DOG FRIENDLINESS•	On leads in reserve, can be free on drove tracks
•PARKING•	Free car park at Decoy Pool, signposted from public road
•PUBLIC TOILETS•	None on route
•NOTE•	To bypass rough part, follow lane between Points ④ and ⑥

BACKGROUND TO THE WALK

At Westhay Moor the Somerset Trust for Nature Conservation (STNC) is carefully recreating the original peat wetland from a time before drainage and peat cuttings. This involves raising the water table with polythene barriers, and importing sphagnum moss and peatland plants from Cumbria. 'True blanket bog', one of their notices reminds us, 'should wobble when walked on...' And while these rehabilitated peat diggings are very good news for waterfowl and the nightjar, for rare spiders and the bog bush cricket, they are still a long way from the original Somerset moor.

Moor or Morass?

'Moor' is the same as 'mire' or 'morass'; the Saxon word first occurs in the account of King Alfred taking refuge at Muchelney. For the Saxons the moor was a place of mystery and fear. About 1,500 years ago the monster Grendel was the original 'Thing from the Swamp' in the poem of *Beowulf*. Open water alternated with reed beds and mud. The inhabitants moved around by boat, or by wading, or on stilts. Even if you could see out over the reeds it rarely helped as the mist would come down. And, at nightfall, the will o' the wisp misled you into the unstable mud, just in case you hadn't been swallowed up in it already.

If you did ever get out on to firm land, you were quite likely to be infected with ague or marsh fever. Even the modern name, 'malaria', reflects its supposed origin in the misty airs of the wetlands. Actually it was transmitted by mosquitoes that bred in the stagnant water. Oliver Cromwell, a fenman from East Anglia, died of malaria. It persisted in the marshes of Essex into the 20th century and may return with global warming in the 21st.

Wet Refuge

For those who knew its ways, the moor was the safest of refuges. Iron Age tribes built a village on wooden piles near Glastonbury; the Romans complained of the way the tribesmen would hide with only their heads above the water. Alfred found safety from the Danes here, as did the monks of Glastonbury.

Wealth in the Wet

The moor was also, in its own way, wealthy. The less wet sections grew a rich summer pasture, fertilised by the silt of the winter floods. It's no coincidence that Britain's most famous cheese comes from the edge of the Levels. The deep, moist soil also grew heavy crops of hemp. Henry VIII made the growing of this useful plant compulsory, as it supplied cordage and sailcloth for the navy. Today, under its Latin name of *Cannabis sativa*, it is, of course, strictly forbidden. The wetter ground yielded osiers for baskets and reed for thatch; wildfowl and fish; and goosefeather quills for penmen. Fuel was peat, or willow poles from the pollarded trees whose roots supported the ditches. And the rent for this desirable property was often paid in live eels.

Walk 7

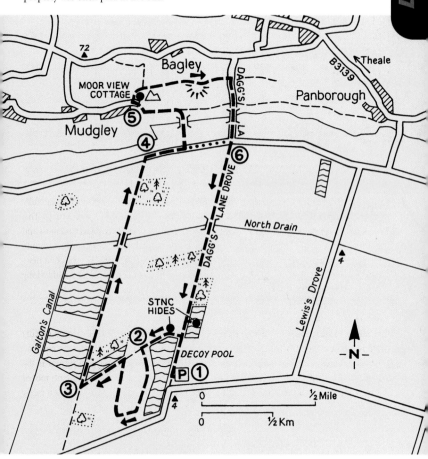

Walk 7 **Directions**

① Head into the reserve on a broad track, with **Decoy Pool** hiding behind reeds on the left. At the end of the lake a kissing gate leads to the STNC hide, with a broad path

continuing between high reedbeds. Ignore a gate on the left ('No Visitor Access') but go through a kissing gate 60yds (55m) further on.

② A fenced track runs through peat ground, where birches are being felled to recreate blanket bog.

Walk 7

The track turns right; now take a
kissing gate on the left for a path
through trees. At its end a new track
leads back through the peat. At the
end turn left to reach a gate on to
the next of the 'droves' or raised
trackways through the peatland.

③ Turn right, passing hides and
crossing a bridge over the wide
North Drain; the land on each side
now comprises water-meadows.
The track leads to a lane.

④ If you wish to omit the field
paths above (which are rough, but
give a splendid view over the
reserve), simply turn right, going
along the road for 650yds (594m)
to a junction, Point ⑥. Otherwise
turn right as far as a right-hand
bend, and continue for 175yds
(160m) to where gates are on both
sides of the road. Go through the
left-hand one (with a red-painted
marker) and cross to a gate and
bridge over a ditch. Follow the left
edge of the next field to its corner.
Turn left through a gate and follow
field edges to a small orchard. Turn
right, up to the end of a tarred lane.

⑤ Turn left along the road to an
uphill path to the left of **Moor View
Cottage** – this becomes overgrown
and quite steep – to a stile on the
right. Cross the tops of five fields.

In the sixth field drop slightly to
pass below farm buildings (there is
a helpful signpost here). A gate
leads into a small orchard, with a
signposted gate on to **Dagg's Lane**
just above. Turn down the lane to
the road below.

⑥ Directly opposite Dagg's Lane is
the track, **Dagg's Lane Drove**. This
runs between meadows then re-
enters the reserve, passing between
pools left by peat extraction. Look
out for a path on the left signposted
to a hide. This leads out excitingly
on stilts above the flooded mire.
Return from the hide and rejoin the
drove track, which quickly leads
back to the car park.

Studland's Sand and Heath

Easy walking through a significant nature reserve over beach and heath.

•DISTANCE•	7 miles (11.3km)
•MINIMUM TIME•	4hrs
•ASCENT / GRADIENT•	132ft (40m)
•LEVEL OF DIFFICULTY•	
•PATHS•	Sandy beach, muddy heathland tracks, verges, no stiles
•LANDSCAPE•	Sandy Studland Bay, heath and views over Poole Harbour
•SUGGESTED MAP•	aqua3 OS Explorer OL 15 Purbeck & South Dorset
•START / FINISH•	Grid reference: SZ 033835
•DOG FRIENDLINESS•	Not allowed on beach June–September, check locally for precise dates
•PARKING•	Knoll car park, by visitor centre, just off B3351
•PUBLIC TOILETS•	By visitor centre and near ferry toll station

BACKGROUND TO THE WALK

The glorious sands in Studland Bay are justly famous, attracting over one million visitors a year, so you'll need to get up early to have the beach to yourself. You're unlikely to be alone for long and local horseriders are often the first to arrive.

Naked Gape

As you progress up the beach, getting warmer, you can shed your clothes with impunity, for the upper stretch is the less familiar form of nature reserve, opening its arms to naturists. Even on a winter's morning you'll spot brave souls sunbathing naked in the shelter of the marram-covered dunes. Off-shore you'll see big, sleek motor boats – of the 'gin palace' variety – letting rip as they emerge from the constraints of Poole Harbour. Watch out, too, for the orange and blue of the Poole lifeboat on practice manoeuvres, and the yellow and black pilot boat nipping out to lead in the tankers. Jet skiers zip around the more sedate sailing yachts, all dodging the small fishing boats. It's a perfect seaside harmony, complete with 'wheedling' gulls.

Studland's sand is pale gold and fine-ground, trodden by thousands of feet, piled into hundreds of satisfying sand castles and smoothed daily by the sea. The shells underfoot become more numerous as you approach the tip of the sand bar. It's a wonderful opportunity for some shell spotting. Look for the flattish conical mother-of-pearl whorls of topshells, the curious pinky-brown pockets of slipper limpets, the glossy, uneven orange disks of the common saddle oyster and the flat reddish-brown sun-rays of scallops. The deeply ridged fans of common cockles and the vivid blue flash of mussels are a common sight. More challenging is to identify the uneven ellipse of sand gapers or the delicate finger-nail pink of the thin tellin.

Behind the beach lies the rugged heath, part of the same nature reserve, which is in the care of English Nature and the National Trust. These two bodies are currently working together on a programme of restoration. They are reclaiming heath that had become farmland, clearing scrub and maintaining controlled grazing to prevent it all reverting to woodland. I saw my first rare Dartford warbler here, perched on a sprig of gorse – with its

Walk 8

pinky brown colouring and long tail, it's a distinctive little bird. All six of Britain's reptiles – common lizard, sand lizard, smooth snake, adder, grass snake and slow-worm – live on the heath. They may be spotted if you know where to look and what you're looking for. Be patient and you might see one soaking up the sunshine in a quiet corner. Trapped between the dunes and the heath is a freshwater lake known as the Little Sea. Hides allow you to watch the dizzying variety of coastal and freshwater birds which congregate here.

Walk 8 Directions

① From the car park go past the **visitor centre** to the sea. Turn left and walk up the beach for about 2 miles (3.2km). Marram-covered dunes hide the edge of the heath on your left, but you have views to Tennyson Down on the Isle of Wight, and the golden cliffs of Bournemouth curve away ahead. Continue round the tip of the sand bar into **Shell Bay**. Poole opens out ahead – more precisely, the spit of Sandbanks, with the gleaming white Haven Hotel facing you across the harbour mouth. There are good views of the tree-covered nature reserve island of Brownsea, with Branksea Castle staring boldly out at the eastern end.

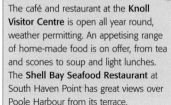

WHERE TO EAT AND DRINK
The café and restaurant at the **Knoll Visitor Centre** is open all year round, weather permitting. An appetising range of home-made food is on offer, from tea and scones to soup and light lunches. The **Shell Bay Seafood Restaurant** at South Haven Point has great views over Poole Harbour from its terrace.

② Turn inland when you reach **South Haven Point**, joining the road by the phone box. Pass the boatyard and toll booth then bear right at a gate on to a bridleway, leading down to some houseboats. Turn left along the tranquil inner shore of **Poole Harbour** and past **Bramble Bush Bay**. Choose any of the various tracks that lead back up to the road. Cross over and follow the verge until the end of some woods on your left, when you can pick up the broad muddy track on the heath. After ½ mile (800m) this bends left, with views across to the Little Sea. Where the track bends sharply right to meet the road, stay straight ahead on the footpath for a few more paces.

FOR BIRDWATCHERS
In addition to this location's speciality, the Dartford warbler, other heathland species include resident stonechats and summer-visiting whitethroats and nightjars. As you pass the shores of Poole Harbour, scrutinise the numerous waders for the occasional spotted redshank, more elegant and longer-billed than its cousin the redshank, which also occurs here in good numbers.

③ Cross the road by a bus stop and head down the track, indicated by a fingerpost. Go past the marshy end

WHILE YOU'RE THERE
A chain **ferry** crosses every few minutes between Sandbanks and South Haven Point, disgorging its 'townies' on to the beach and its cars to hurry off into Portland. From Sandbanks you can catch a ferry, spring and summer, to **Brownsea Island**. Red squirrels are the best-known inhabitants of this 494 acre (200ha) nature reserve, but the lagoon supports an important ternery, and avocets, ruff and other unusual waders are regular visitors. There are many other rare creatures to discover, including 17 species of dragonfly and an endangered species of ant.

of **Studland Heath** and up to a junction by **Greenland Farm**. Bear left and, just round the next corner, turn left through a gate on to the heath. Go straight along an old hedge-line, pass a barn on the left, and reach a fingerpost.

④ Turn left across the heath (not shown on the fingerpost), aiming for the distant lump of the **Agglestone**. Go through a gate by another fingerpost and continue along the

muddy track over the top, passing the Agglestone away to your right. Go down into some woods, turn right over a footbridge and pass through a gate into a lane.

Pass several houses then, where blue markers indicate a public bridleway, turn left into a field. Head diagonally right into a green lane and go through a gate at the bottom. Turn left along the verge, pass the Knoll House Hotel and turn right at the signpost to return to the car park.

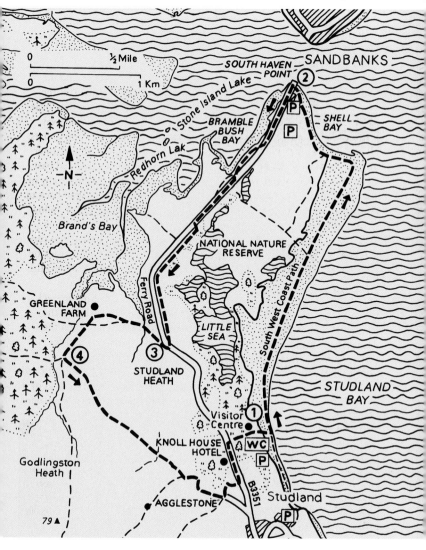

Vale of Pewsey and Oare Hill

Combine a gentle canalside stroll with a stiff downland climb to the summit of Oare Hill for magnificent views across the Vale of Pewsey.

•DISTANCE•	5 miles (8km)
•MINIMUM TIME•	2hrs 15min
•ASCENT / GRADIENT•	393ft (120m) ▲▲▲
•LEVEL OF DIFFICULTY•	🚶 🚶 🚶
•PATHS•	Tow path, tracks, field paths, lanes, 4 stiles
•LANDSCAPE•	Vale of Pewsey and chalk downland
•SUGGESTED MAP•	aqua3 OS Explorer 157 Marlborough & Savernake Forest
•START / FINISH•	Grid reference: SU 157610
•DOG FRIENDLINESS•	Let off lead along tow path
•PARKING•	Free car park at Pewsey Wharf
•PUBLIC TOILETS•	None on route

Walk 9 Directions

The Vale of Pewsey separates Wiltshire's two principle areas of chalk downland, Salisbury Plain to the south and the Marlborough Downs to the north. Through its heart meanders the Kennet and Avon Canal, the longest and most important of the canals within Wiltshire, built between 1794 and 1810 to link the River Kennet, which flows into the Thames at Reading, with the River Avon at Bath. It was used to carry iron, coal, stone and timber from Bristol and to bring luxuries like tobacco and spirits from London. The canal company built the wharf at Pewsey to serve the village, but it was never a great commercial success and was eclipsed by those at nearby Burbage to the east and Honey Street to the west. It remains much as it was in the past. The main buildings consists of a cottage, which would have housed the wharfinger – owner or keeper – of the wharf, and the two-storey warehouse, used to store goods transported by canal.

Facing the canal, turn right along the tow path and walk beside the canal for just over a mile (1.6km) to the second bridge. Cross the stile on your right before the bridge and turn left along the lane, crossing the canal bridge. At a road junction, keep ahead towards downland. Pass cottages on your right and proceed ahead through the gateway along the drive. Where this bears left to **West Wick House**, continue straight on along the grass-centred track,

FOR BIRDWATCHERS

On this walk of contrasts, you are likely to encounter open country birds such as kestrel and skylark on the downs, with common buzzard an increasingly frequent sight in recent years. By contrast, the wetlands bordering the River Avon are home to reed buntings and sedge warblers during the summer months and water rails in winter; listen for the pig-like squeals of the latter.

Walk 9

which soon narrows and begins to climb steadily towards **Martinsell Hill**. Go through a gate and bear left at the fork to ascend a steep sunken lane (this can be muddy). At the top, keep left of the gate, disregard the waymarked stile on your right and bear left alongside the fence, following a path towards the long barrow on the summit of **Oare Hill**.

The Giants Grave is an ancient unchambered burial site that has a charming legend associated with it. It is claimed that the giant will stir from his slumbers if anyone runs around the tomb seven times. Standing as it does on the top of Oare Hill, it is a splendid vantage point from which to savour far-reaching views across the Vale of Pewsey and the North Wessex Downs. You can also see the impressive combes and dry valleys etched into the downland scarp slopes away to your right. The unimproved chalk downlands along the steep escarpment of the vale and on nearby Martinsell Hill are noted for their extremely rich chalk grassland flora, notably cowslip, burnt orchid and devil's bit scabious, and a wide variety of butterflies including Adonis and chalkhill blue and dark green fritillary butterflies.

Follow the path past the trig point and descend the steep grassy slope towards **Oare**, soon to reach a stile at the bottom. Bear left along the field edge and follow the path across the field to a gate and crossing of ways. Take the footpath ahead, bearing right, then left around the field edge to reach a lane. Cross the stile opposite and bear half-left across the field to a stile. Cut across the field corner to a further stile and turn right along a track. Keep ahead where it bears right towards a farm and continue to the **Kennet and Avon Canal**. Cross the bridge and bear left back down to rejoin the tow path, passing **Jones's Mill – The Vera Jeans Nature Reserve**.

Bordering the River Avon and fed by numerous springs, this wetland reserve, or fen, is a rare environment within Wiltshire and an exciting place because of the diverse wildlife it supports. Since the water-meadows were abandoned, the site has developed an exceptionally rich flora with 14 species of sedge (a grass-like plant) alone. Dotted among the sedge you will also find bogbean, bog pimpernel and southern marsh orchid. An unusual sight are the belted Galloway cattle which graze the fen to keep the coarser vegetation at bay, thus allowing the more delicate flowers to thrive. The wet woodland in the middle of the reserve has an understorey of huge tussock sedges and great horsetails creating a prehistoric landscape. Retrace your steps back to the car park at **Pewsey Wharf**.

Westbury White Horse

An exhilarating downland walk to a famous white horse..

•DISTANCE•	4 miles (6.4km)
•MINIMUM TIME•	2hrs 30min
•ASCENT / GRADIENT•	557ft (170m) ▲▲▲
•LEVEL OF DIFFICULTY•	林 林 林
•PATHS•	Field paths and downland tracks, 1 stile
•LANDSCAPE•	Downland
•SUGGESTED MAP•	aqua3 OS Explorer 143 Warminster & Trowbridge
•START / FINISH•	Grid reference: ST 914523
•DOG FRIENDLINESS•	Let dogs off lead on top of Westbury Hill
•PARKING•	Jubilee Hall in Tynings Lane, Bratton, just off B3098
•PUBLIC TOILETS•	None on route

Walk 10 **Directions**

The most notable feature of Bratton, a large modern village in the shadow of a huge downland escarpment, is the Church of St James the Great, arguably one of the most charming churches in the county. Reached by a series of steep steps, and nestling at the base of the chalk downland, it dates from the 13th century and is worth the climb to view the traces of Norman architecture and the wildly grinning gargoyles.

Turn right out of the car park to the **B3098**. Turn left, then almost immediately left again up **Butts Lane**. Fork right into **Upper Garston Lane** by the **Oratory of St Giles** then, just before the lane dips, take the path left, waymarked

---

WHERE TO EAT AND DRINK ⓘ

Refresh yourselves after this taxing downland walk at the **Duke** in Bratton, noted for its generous home-cooked food, including excellent Sunday roasts, and Moles ales.

---

to the church. Descend steps, cross a brook, then climb steps to the church gates. Take the narrow path right and ascend through trees. Ignore the stile on your left and climb the stile ahead into pasture at the base of downland.

Follow the permissive path half-right up the field, passing through a belt of trees, then climb diagonally up the scarp slope to the fence at the top. Keep right alongside the fence, go through a gate, then turn right through a metal gate to follow a sunken track around the top of **Combe Bottom**. At the lane, turn left uphill and soon take the track, right, on to the outer rampart of **Bratton Camp**. Bear right to follow the outer rampart path to reach the **Westbury White Horse** hill figure.

Westbury Hill rises to the commanding height of 750ft (229m) above sea level and forms the dramatic western edge of Salisbury Plain. The views are tremendous, with the scarp slope dropping into the Vale of Pewsey, and on the horizon, on a clear day,

Walk 10

you can see across Somerset to the Mendips and the Cotswolds. Dominating the hilltop is Bratton Castle, an Iron-Age hill fort covering 25 acres (10ha) of the plateau and defended by double banks and ditches rising to 35ft (11m). The long barrow inside the fort is a burial mound probably built before 3000 BC.

Cut into the side of the hill, just below the castle ramparts, is Wiltshire's oldest and best known white horse measuring 180ft (55m) long and 108ft (33m) high. This graceful hill figure is believed to have replaced a much earlier and cruder creature which local tradition states was cut in celebration of King Alfred's victory over the Danes at the Battle of Ethundun in AD 878. The present, well-proportioned animal, which is featured on the bottles of a brand of whisky of the same name, was cut

by a Mr Gee, steward to Lord Abingdon, in 1778, apparently because he objected to the primitive dog-like creature which had previously existed on Westbury Hill. The White Horse was remodelled in 1853 and restored 20 years later, with its most recent makeover in concrete, courtesy of Westbury Cement Works. This is the unmistakable industrial complex you can see in the valley below.

Shortly, leave the rampart and pass through a gate on to **Westbury Hill**. Keep to the path, passing benches and a viewpoint pillar, and soon reach a track. Turn left, pass the car park entrance and turn right at the T-junction. Pass **White Horse Farm** and turn left along the track to join the **Imber Range Perimeter Path**.

This is a 30 mile (48km) trail circumnavigating the Army's largest live firing range in the south of England. For over 50 years an area of Salisbury Plain 10 miles (16.1km) long and 5 miles (8km) wide has been occupied by the Army and public access has been very limited. Your view south is across the great central plateau, a wild and lonely landscape, full of mystery and a sense of space.

Keep to the track for ¾ mile (1.2km) to a barn and take the bridle path left through a gate. Follow the track past a copse into a field and keep to the left-hand edge to a gate. Bear right steeply down a sunken track towards **Bratton**. Go through a gate and descend through trees and keep ahead on reaching a metalled lane. Turn left at the T-junction, then bear left up a cobbled path (**The Ball**) between cottages. At the road, keep left back to the hall and car park.

Walk 11

New Forest Trails

Ancient oaks, historic inclosures and exotic towering conifers in the New Forest.

•DISTANCE•	6 miles (9.7km)
•MINIMUM TIME•	3hrs
•ASCENT / GRADIENT•	210ft (64m) ▲ ⏶ ⏶
•LEVEL OF DIFFICULTY•	🚶 🚶 🚶
•PATHS•	Grass and gravel forest tracks, heathland paths, some roads
•LANDSCAPE•	Ornamental Drive, ancient forest inclosures and heathland
•SUGGESTED MAP•	aqua3 OS Outdoor Leisure 22 New Forest
•START / FINISH•	Grid reference: SU 266057
•DOG FRIENDLINESS•	Keep dogs under control at all times
•PARKING•	Brock Hill Forestry Commission car park, just off A35
•PUBLIC TOILETS•	Blackwater car park

BACKGROUND TO THE WALK

A short drive south west of Lyndhurst are ancient woods of oak and beech, notably Bolderwood, and the impressive, mid-19th century conifer plantation of the Rhinefield Ornamental Drive. Here you are in the true heart of the New Forest and this fascinating loop walk explores these contrasting landscapes. The shorter loop (Walk 12) is a relaxing stroll through the rhododendron-lined Ornamental Drive, with its magnificent tall trees and arboretum, while this walk takes you through the forest's finest unenclosed and 'inclosed' deciduous woods. Link the two together for a memorable 8 mile (12.9km) ramble.

Finest Relics of Woodland

Unenclosed woodlands such as Brinken Wood and Gritnam Wood are among the finest relics of unspoilt deciduous forest in Western Europe. Hummocky green lawns and paths meander beneath giant beech trees and beside stands of ancient holly and contorted oaks, and through peaceful, sunny glades edged with elegant silver birch. 'Inclosures' are areas of managed woodlands where young trees are protected from deer and ponies. Areas of oak trees were first inclosed in the late 17th century to provide the huge quantities of timber required by the construction and shipbuilding industries. Holidays Hill Inclosure is one of the forest's oldest, dating from 1676. Here you'll find some 300-year-old oak trees that matured after iron replaced wood in the shipbuilding industry.

You will pass the most famous and probably the oldest tree in the forest, the Knightwood Oak, soon after beginning the longer walk. It is thought to be at least 350 years old and owes its great age to pollarding (cutting back) its limbs to encourage new branches for fuel and charcoal. Pollarding was made illegal in 1698 as full-grown trees were needed to provide timber for shipbuilding, so any oak or beech tree that show signs of having been pollarded is of a great age. Marvel at the girth of this fine oak, a massive 23ft (7m), before walking through Holidays Hill Inclosure to view two of the forest's best-known sites.

Close to Millyford Bridge and Highland Water stands the Portugese Fireplace, a memorial to the work of a Portugese Army unit, deployed during the First World War to cut timber for pit-props. The flint fireplace was used in their cookhouse. Returning through Holidays Hill Inclosure you will join a 'reptile trail' and several marker posts, each carved with a different type of British reptile, lead you to the New Forest reptillary. Set up to breed rarer species for the wild, including the smooth snake and sand lizard, it offers you the opportunity to view some of the forest's more elusive inhabitants. Visit on a hot sunny day, when these cold blooded creatures are more active, and you will see the venomous adder, the olive green grass snake, common lizards and the rare Natterjack toad. Snake catching was once an important trade in the forest during the 19th century and the most celebrated snakecatcher was Brusher Mills, who lived in a hut in Gritnam Wood for over 30 years. It is believed he caught around 35,000 snakes in his time, selling them to zoos and for medicine. He died in 1905 and you will find his grave in Brockenhurst churchyard.

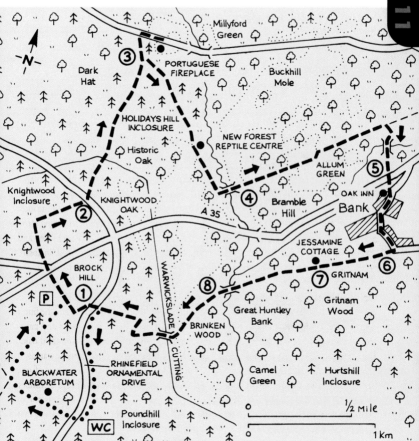

Walk 11 Directions

① Take the gravel path at the southern end of the car park (beyond the information post), parallel with the road. In 100yds (91m) turn right (by a post) and descend to a gravel track. Cross straight over then, where it curves left, keep ahead to a gate and the A35. Cross over, go through a gate and keep to the path, uphill to a junction. Turn right and follow the path to a road. Cross into **Knightwood Oak** car park and follow the sign to the **Knightwood Oak** itself.

Walk 11

② Return to the car park, bear right, then immediately right again by a fallen tree on to a path into mixed forest. Cross a stream and soon reach a gravel track. Bear right and keep to this trail, passing **Reptile Trail** markers, to a fork. Keep left and shortly reach a gate and road. Turn right to view the **Portuguese Fireplace**.

③ Return through **Holidays Hill Inclosure** to the fork of tracks. Bear left and follow this to the **New Forest Reptile Centre**. Walk along the access drive, passing **Holiday Hills Cottage** then, at a barrier on your left, drop down on to a path and follow it across a bridge.

WHERE TO EAT AND DRINK ⓘ
You may well find an **ice cream van** in Blackwater car park on Walk 11. On Walk 12, aim to make it to the **Oak** in Bank for lunch. A traditional pub, it offers ale from the cask, and decent food.

---

④ Keep to the main path for ¾ mile (1.2km), skirting the walls to **Allum Green** and several clearings, then gently climb through trees to a defined crossing of paths and turn right. Shortly, bear half-right across a clearing and concrete footbridge, then continue through the woodland edge to a telegraph pole. Bear right for 20yds (18m), then left through a gate to the A35.

⑤ Turn left, then almost immediately right across the road to a gate. Walk ahead to a garden boundary and turn right, the narrow path leading to a lane in **Bank**. Turn right, pass the **Oak Inn** and walk through the hamlet. Just before a sharp left-hand bend (by a cattle-grid), bear off right beside a barrier and walk straight ahead on a wide path.

FOR BIRDWATCHERS 🐦
Woodland birds predominate on this walk, with species highlights varying throughout the year. Migrant redstarts and wood warblers are present from May to August. Although here all year round, chaffinches build up in winter and it is worth scrutinising sizeable flocks at this time of year for the occasional brambling – a winter visitor from northern Europe.

---

⑥ Go through trees and scrub to a fork on the edge of a clearing. Keep right to follow the path between an oak and a holly tree. Negotiate a boggy area, then at a fork, keep left and follow the path to a metalled lane at **Gritnam**.

⑦ Continue ahead, pass **Jessamine Cottage** then, where it bends right, keep ahead across rough grassland into trees. Bear slightly right and walk alongside a thick birch copse. Remain on the path (ill-defined in places as it skirts fallen trees), and eventually join a wide grassy path. Turn left and continue to a bridge.

⑧ Ignore the path immediately left, keep ahead between a tree and an old fallen branch to follow the path through **Brinken Wood**. Enter a clearing and keep ahead to cross a bridge over **Warwickslade Cutting**. At a gravel track, turn right, then take the first path left and soon merge with the start of the **Tall Trees Trail**, opposite **Brock Hill** car park.

WHILE YOU'RE THERE ⓘ
Visit the **New Forest Museum and Visitor Centre** in Lyndhurst which brings to life the history, traditions and wildlife of the New Forest. Take a trip up the **Bolderwood Ornamental Drive** and visit the **deer sanctuary** near Bolderwood car park. Specially-constructed platforms offer an intimate view of the deer.

Rhinefield Ornamental Drive

A short loop round the impressive 19th-century plantation.
See map and information panel for Walk 11

•DISTANCE•	2 miles (3.2km)
•MINIMUM TIME•	1hr
•ASCENT / GRADIENT•	49ft (15m) ▲ ▲ ▲
•LEVEL OF DIFFICULTY•	🚶 🚶 🚶

Walk 12 Directions
(See Walk 11 map)

At the bottom of **Rhinefield Ornamental Drive** stands the **Rhinefield House Hotel**, a flamboyant Jacobean-style house, built in 1890 on the site of a hunting lodge used by Charles II. Magnificent gardens surround the mansion and rhododendrons and azaleas line the ornamental carriage drive, until 1938 a gravel track, that links the house with the A35. Planted informally in the mid 19th century with exotic trees such as Wellingtonias and redwoods, Ornamental Drive has reached maturity and some of the trees are the largest of their species in Britain. This short circular trail passes some of these specimens.

Locate the **Tall Trees Trail** post at the southern end of the car park and follow the gravel path to the road and cross straight over. Keep to the gravel trail (marked by red-banded posts) as it curves right and runs parallel with the road. Pass through a mixed wooded area, featuring tall Douglas firs, one of which is over 150ft (46m) tall and Norwegian spruces. The path meanders gently downhill to **Blackwater** car park, passing the remains of a ditch and bank along the way. Rhinefield was first inclosed in 1700 and this section of the original bank and pale fence represents part of the first Inclosure boundary.

Make for the car park entrance and cross the road, signed '**Blackwater Arboretum**'. Shortly, turn right if you wish to explore the **Tall Trees Trail** further and return to the track. Turn right and go through a gate into the arboretum. Although not a large area, it is well worth exploring the various paths that criss-cross the arboretum, passing labelled trees and welcome benches, where you can rest and enjoy the peace and quiet. Exit by the far gate and keep to the gravel track to a crossing of tracks. Turn right and remain on this track to a second crossing of paths. (Turn left to join Walk 11). Turn right uphill, then on reaching a gravel path, turn left back to the car park.

FOR BIRDWATCHERS

This is something of a hotspot for birdwatchers seeking speciality woodland birds like lesser spotted woodepecker, hawfinch and crossbill. All three species are present throughout the year although easiest to see in winter when leaves have fallen from the deciduous trees. The latter two species sometimes visit puddles on the ground to drink.

Walk 13

Newtown and its estuary

Discover the fascinating history of the island's former capital and the excellent birdlife on the salt marshes and creeks of the Newtown estuary.

•DISTANCE•	3½ miles (5.6km)
•MINIMUM TIME•	2hrs
•ASCENT / GRADIENT•	85ft (25m)
•LEVEL OF DIFFICULTY•	
•PATHS•	Tracks, field paths, raised dykes and some roads, 4 stiles
•LANDSCAPE•	Gently rolling farmland, woodland and salt marsh
•SUGGESTED MAP•	aqua3 OS Outdoor Leisure 29 Isle of Wight
•START / FINISH•	Grid reference: SZ 413894
•DOG FRIENDLINESS•	Keep dogs under control
•PARKING•	Shalfleet village car park, off A3054
•PUBLIC TOILETS•	None on route

Walk 13 Directions

Shalfleet developed where the Caul Bourne widens into a creek at the head of the Newtown estuary. Take a look at the church with its impressive, fort-like tower, built in the 11th century with 5ft (1.5m) thick walls and used as a refuge from French invaders during the 14th century, and stroll out to the small 17th-century quay, once busy with boats unloading coal or taking on corn and now popular with yachts and sailing dinghies.

Turn left out of the car park, then right at the fork down **Mill Road** to pass **Shalfleet Mill**. Cross the footbridge and follow the path up through woodland to a metalled drive. Bear left and follow the drive to a road. Turn left and keep to the road for 200yds (183m) to a gate and permissive path on your left. Keep to the right-hand edge of two fields, parallel with the road, to a

gate. Turn left, then left again along **Town Lane**, signed to **Newtown**. Cross the bridge at the head of **Causeway Lake** and take the path left over a stile. Walk along the edge of the tidal creek to a stile, then along the edge of **Hay Meadow**. Keep to the path as it bears right to a gate to join a tree-lined path leading into **Newtown**.

The most ancient of the island boroughs, Francheville, as Newtown was once known, was the island's capital, being founded by the Bishop of Winchester in 1218. Situated on the Newtown River estuary, it developed into a major seaport, with great, masted ships dwarfing bustling quays and trade

---

WHERE TO EAT AND DRINK ⓘ

The welcoming, 200-year-old **New Inn** at Shalfleet boasts flagstoned floors, a huge open fireplace, scrubbed pine tables, a good range of ales, and an interesting menu that specialises in fresh local fish. There's also a sheltered rear garden.

Walk 13

thriving with local salt and oysters. Its streets were designed on a grid system and their names recall the medieval merchants and craftsmen – Gold Street, Drapers Alley – although most are now only grassy lanes. All this changed in 1377 when the town was burnt down by a combined French and Spanish raid. It was never fully rebuilt, although the town hall was rebuilt in 1699 and until 1832 it returned two Members of Parliament.

Today, Newtown, which has no through traffic, is a tranquil place and best explored on foot. You can wander along a network of footpaths through the old streets and visit the beautifully restored Victorian church, and the isolated town hall where you can learn more about the history of this fascinating place.

At the lane, keep ahead and follow it left to pass a parking area. Take the path through a gate beside the **Old Coastguard Station**. Beyond a further gate, keep to the left-hand edge of the meadow to a gate and follow the raised path alongside the estuary.

Perhaps surprisingly, the windswept salt marshes and mudflats were only created in their present form as late as 1954, following a violent winter storm which breached the sea wall.

Bordering shallow creeks and the estuary, it is a magical place, and a paradise for both birds and birdwatchers. Wildfowl and waders abound here. Oystercatchers and redshanks probe the mudflats for morsels, a variety of ducks dabble in the shallows, nesting gulls squabble on Gull Island, and common and little terns gracefully glide through the shimmering summer air, while flocks of geese wheel overhead in winter, and always and everywhere you will hear the evocative bubbling call of the curlew. For a small fee you can visit the bird reserve and watch from well positioned hides.

Continue to the sheds at **Newtown Quay**, then head inland across the narrow jetty to a gate. In a few paces turn left and follow the footpath towards the bird hide. Bear right inland to a drive and the lane. Turn left, cross the stile on your left and proceed behind the houses to a stile and lane. Turn right, pass the old town hall and follow the lane down to the bridge at **Causeway Lake**. From here retrace your steps back to **Shalfleet Mill** and the car park. An enjoyable extra mile (1.6km) can be added by following the footpath you'll see right at the end of **Mill Lane**. Walk along the track parallel with the tidal **Shalfleet Lake** to **Shalfleet Quay** for a different view of **Newtown River** and its tidal creeks.

Walk 14

The Snake River and the Seven Sisters

Follow a breezy trail beside the Cuckmere River as it winds in erratic fashion towards the sea.

•DISTANCE•	3 miles (4.8km)
•MINIMUM TIME•	1hr 30min
•ASCENT / GRADIENT•	Negligible
•LEVEL OF DIFFICULTY•	
•PATHS•	Grassy trails and well-used paths. Mostly beside the Cuckmere or canalised branch of river
•LANDSCAPE•	Exposed and isolated valley and river mouth
•SUGGESTED MAP•	aqua3 OS Explorer 123 South Downs Way – Newhaven to Eastbourne
•START / FINISH•	Grid reference: TV 518995
•DOG FRIENDLINESS•	Under close control within Seven Sisters Country Park. On lead during lambing season and near A259
•PARKING•	Fee-paying car park at Seven Sisters Country Park
•PUBLIC TOILETS•	Opposite car park, by visitor centre

BACKGROUND TO THE WALK

One of the few remaining undeveloped river mouths in the south-east, is the gap or cove known as Cuckmere Haven. It is one of the south coast's best-known and most popular beauty spots and was regularly used by smugglers in the 18th century to bring ashore their cargoes of brandy and lace. The scene has changed very little in the intervening years with the eternal surge of waves breaking on the isolated shore.

The Cuckmere River joins the English Channel at this point but not before it makes a series of extraordinarily wide loops through lush water-meadows. It's hardly surprising that this characteristic has earned it the occasional epithet 'Snake River'. Winding ever closer to the sea, the Cuckmere emerges beside the famous white chalk cliffs known as the Seven Sisters. Extending east towards Birling Gap, there are, in fact, eight of these towering chalk faces, with the highest one, Haven Brow (253ft/77m), closest to the river mouth. On the other side of the estuary rise the cliffs of Seaford Head, a nature reserve run by the local authority.

Seven Sisters Country Park

The focal point of the lower valley is the Seven Sisters Country Park, an amenity area of 692 acres (280ha) developed by East Sussex County Council. The site is a perfect location for a country park and has been imaginatively planned to blend with the coastal beauty of this fascinating area. There are artificial lakes and park trails, and an old Sussex barn near by has been converted to provide a visitor centre which includes many interesting exhibits and displays.

However, there is more to the park than these obvious attractions. Wildlife plays a key role within the park's boundaries, providing naturalists with many hours of pleasure and enjoyment. The flowers and insects found here are at their best in early to mid summer, while spring and autumn are a good time to bring your binoculars with you for a close-up view of migrant birds.

A Haven for Birds

Early migrant wheatears are sometimes spotted in the vicinity of the river mouth from late February onwards and are followed later in the season by martins, swallows, whinchats and warblers. Keep a careful eye out for whitethroats, terns and waders too. The lakes and lagoons tend to attract waders such as curlews, sandpipers and little stints. Grey phalaropes have also been seen in the park, usually after severe autumn storms. These elusive birds spend most of their lives far out to sea, usually off South America or western Africa.

The walk explores this part of the Cuckmere Valley and begins by heading for the beach. As you make your way there, you might wonder why the river meanders the way it does. The meltwaters of the last Ice Age shaped this landscape and over the centuries rising sea levels and a freshwater peat swamp influenced the river's route to the Channel. Around the start of the 19th century, the sea rose to today's level and a new straight cut with raised banks, devised in 1846, shortened the Cuckmere's journey. This unnatural waterway controls the river and helps prevent flooding in the valley.

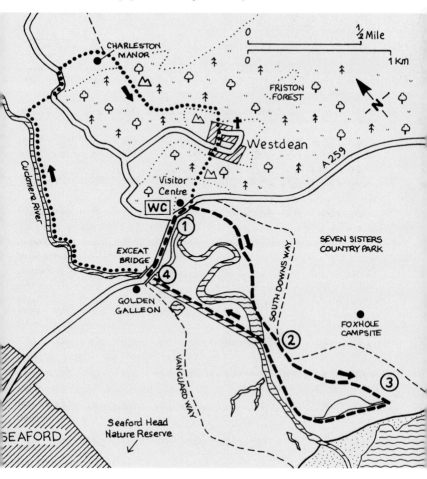

Walk 14 Directions

① Make for the gate near the entrance to the **Seven Sisters Country Park** and follow the wide, grassy path towards the beach. The path gradually curves to the right, running alongside a concrete track. The **Cuckmere River** meanders beside you, heading for the open sea. Continue ahead between the track and the river and make for a **South Downs Way** sign.

WHERE TO EAT AND DRINK

The **Golden Galleon** by Exceat Bridge is a popular 18th-century inn thought to have inspired Rudyard Kipling's poem *Song of the Smugglers*. The menu is traditional English, with various Italian, Oriental and Indian dishes. The ales are supplied by the pub's own micro-brewery. The visitor centre at the **Seven Sisters Country Park** has a restaurant and tea rooms and in summer there is often an ice cream van in the car park.

---

② Avoid the long distance trail as it runs in from the left, pass it and the **Foxhole campsite** and keep ahead, through the gate towards the beach. Veer left at the beach and **South Downs Way** sign. On reaching the next gate, don't go through it. Instead, keep right and follow the beach sign. Pass a couple of wartime pill boxes on the left, an evocative reminder of less peaceful times, and go through a gate. Join a stony path and walk ahead to the beach, with the white wall of the **Seven Sisters** rearing up beside you.

WHAT TO LOOK FOR

Shingle plants thrive on the sheltered parts of beaches and a stroll at Cuckmere Haven reveals the yellow horned-poppy and the fleshy leaved sea kale. Sea beet, curled dock and scentless chamomile also grow here.

FOR BIRDWATCHERS

Although a greater variety of birds can probably be seen in spring and autumn there is still plenty to see in the height of summer – skylarks, whitethroats, stonechats and yellowhammer are found on the slopes above the Haven. And in harsh winter weather wildfowl and waders often congregate beside the brackish waters when inland freshwater sites become frozen; jack snipe are a highlight at this time.

---

③ Turn right and cross the shore, approaching a **Cuckmere Haven Emergency Point** sign. Branch off to the right to join another track here. Follow this for about 50yds (46m) until you come to a junction and keep left, following the **Habitat Trail** and **Park Trail**. Keep beside the Cuckmere and the landscape here is characterised by a network of meandering channels and waterways, all feeding into the river. Pass a turning for **Foxhole campsite** and follow the footpath as it veers left, in line with the **Cuckmere**. Make for a kissing gate and continue on the straight path by the side of the river.

WHILE YOU'RE THERE

If you have the time, take a look at the **Seaford Head Nature Reserve**, which lies on the west side of Cuckmere Haven. This chalk headland, which rises 282 ft (85m) above the sea, is a popular local attraction and from here the coastal views are magnificent.

---

④ Keep ahead to the road at **Exceat Bridge** and on the left is the **Golden Galleon** pub. Turn right and follow the A259 to return to the car park at the country park.

Cuckmere River and Charleston Manor

A longer walk up the Cuckmere Valley to a 12th-century manor house and the quiet village of Westdean.
See map and information panel for Walk 14

•DISTANCE•	5¾ miles (9.3km)
•MINIMUM TIME•	3hrs
•ASCENT / GRADIENT•	262ft (80m)
•LEVEL OF DIFFICULTY•	
•LANDSCAPE•	Valley and thick woodland, 6 stiles
•DOG FRIENDLINESS•	Several stretches of road. Under control in Friston Forest

To make a longer walk in the Cuckmere Valley, cross **Exceat Bridge** at Point ④ and continue beside the Cuckmere, following the riverside path through this delightful, though lonely, valley. Swans may be seen gliding on the water. Head for a kissing gate, continue over several stiles and look for a path on the right, before a stile.

Take the path away from the **Cuckmere**, following it between trees and bushes. Cross a stile and turn left at the road. Pass the entrance to **Charleston Manor** and as you do so look for the sign on the wall which states this is not Charleston Farmhouse, home of the Bloomsbury Group. Pevsner described this Charleston as 'a perfect house in a perfect setting.' It dates from the early 12th century and has splendid gardens.

Continue for a few paces and turn right to join a path signposted 'Jevington'. Merge with the **South Downs Way** and the **Vanguard Way** and keep right at the fork. Climb the steps and follow the path first south, then south east through

Friston Forest. Veer left at the fork and cut through beech woodland to a clear junction.

Turn right here and make for the hamlet of **Westdean,** lying half-hidden in a wooded hollow. The church dates from the 14th century. Join the road on a bend and go on ahead to a junction. Cross over and walk ahead to a flight of steps.

Make for a stone stile at the top of the steps, where there are views of the **Cuckmere River** winding to the sea. This has to be one of the most dramatic views in Sussex. Descend the steep hillside and make for a kissing gate by the visitor centre. Cross the road and return to the car park.

FOR BIRDWATCHERS

Listen out for sedge warblers and reed buntings as you walk beside the Cuckmere River during spring and summer. While admiring the view of the serpentine river from below Westdean, watch out for birds of prey in flight. Kestrels and sparrowhawks are regularly seen but who knows what else might turn up!

Walk 16

Views and Yews at Kingley Vale

Discover a magical ancient forest and allow your imagination to run riot on this exhilarating walk high up on the South Downs.

•DISTANCE•	5 miles (8km)
•MINIMUM TIME•	2hrs
•ASCENT / GRADIENT•	440ft (134m) ▲▲▲
•LEVEL OF DIFFICULTY•	🚶 🚶 🚶
•PATHS•	Mostly woodland paths and downland tracks
•LANDSCAPE•	Dense woodland and rolling downland
•SUGGESTED MAP•	aqua3 OS Explorer 120 Chichester, South Harting & Selsey
•START / FINISH•	Grid reference: SZ 814215
•DOG FRIENDLINESS•	Under control in Stoughton village. Elsewhere off lead unless signs state otherwise
•PARKING•	Free car park at Stoughton Down
•PUBLIC TOILETS•	None on route

BACKGROUND TO THE WALK

You might not expect to find the largest yew forest in Europe at the western extremity of the South Downs, but that's exactly where it is. This remote downland landscape, covering more than 200 acres (81ha) is cloaked with 30,000 yew trees. Once a wartime artillery range, Kingley Vale became one of Britain's first nature reserves in 1952. Today, it is managed by English Nature.

Gnarled and Twisted Trunks

Silent, isolated and thankfully inaccessible by car, the grove is a haven for ramblers and naturalists. Our walk skirts the forest but if you have the time to explore this enchanting place, then study the map closely and make up your own route. The effort is certainly worthwhile.

The yew is one of our finest trees and can live up to 2,000 years. It is usually a large but squat tree, its branches and dark green needles conspiring to create a dense evergreen canopy which allows little light to filter through to the forest floor. With their deep red trunks, branches and shallow roots twisted into monstrous shapes and gargoyle faces, some of the yews at Kingley Vale are thought to be at least 500 years old.

Even on the sunniest summer's day, the scene amid the tangle of boughs is eerily dark, strange and mystical, like something from the pages of a classic children's fairy story. The yew has always featured strongly in folklore and, according to legend, this place was a meeting point for witches who engaged in pagan rites and wove magical spells here. Danes and Druids are also believed to haunt the vale.

Various theories about the origin of the forest have been suggested but it is thought that the site marks the spot where a 9th-century battle against the Vikings took place. Some sources suggest the trees were planted here to guide pilgrims travelling across the South Downs to Canterbury. Long before the yews began to grow, Bronze Age kings were buried

Walk 16

here, confirmed by various tumuli on the map.

The trees may be the dominant feature at Kingley Vale but the grove is teeming with wildlife. The delightful green woodpecker, noted for its distinctive colouring, inhabits the reserve, one of 57 species of breeding bird found here. The bee orchid blooms in June while mountain sheep and wild fallow deer keep the turf short for 200 other species of flower. If you're lucky, you might spot a fox or a kestrel.

Beginning just outside the village of Stoughton, the walk immediately makes for dense woodland before climbing quite steeply to the spectacular viewpoint overlooking Kingley Vale. The reserve, renowned for its ecological importance, covers the southern chalk slopes of 655ft (206m) high Bow Hill and from this high ground the views are tremendous.

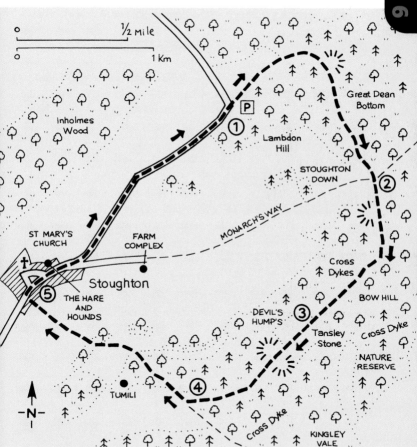

Walk 16 Directions

① From the car park make for the bridleway near the exit and follow it away from the road, skirting dense beech woodland. There are striking views on the left over pastoral, well-wooded countryside. Keep right at a fork and follow the stony path as it curves to the right. Veer right at the next waymarked fork and begin a gradual ascent beneath the boughs of beech trees.

Walk 16

② Eventually you break cover from the trees at a major junction of waymarked tracks. Go straight on, looking to the right for spectacular views. Continue to the next bridleway sign at a fork and join a path running parallel to the track. Cut between trees and keep going until you reach a gap on the right. Keep to the waymarked path as it runs down the slope. Rejoin the enclosed track, turning left to follow it up the slope towards **Bow Hill**.

> ### FOR BIRDWATCHERS
> Although the mysterious, ancient yew trees may not harbour many birds, areas of scrub on the chalk slopes are home to a much greater variety. Yellowhammers and dunnocks are present all year but, in spring and summer, listen for the songs of migrant visiting whitethroats, lesser whitethroats, blackcaps and willow warblers.

③ On reaching the **Devil's Humps**, veer off the path to enjoy the magnificent vistas across the Downland countryside. The view to the north, over remote woodland and downland, is impressive enough, but the panorama to the south is particularly outstanding. Immediately below you are the trees of **Kingley Vale**. Head along the footpath in a westerly direction, with the nature reserve on your left. Continue between carpets of bracken and lines of beech trees.

> ### WHILE YOU'RE THERE ⓘ
> Visit Stoughton's 11th-century cruciform **Church of St Mary**. The exterior is barn-like, bulky even, and inside it is unexpectedly spacious. The south transept was converted into a tower in the 14th century, the nave is over 30ft (9m) high and there is a striking Norman arch with a triple layer of roll mouldings.

> ### WHERE TO EAT AND DRINK ⓘ
> Have a picnic at the Stoughton Down car park or stop off towards the end of the walk at the **Hare and Hounds** in Stoughton. This striking flint building dates back to around the 17th century and was originally built as two cottages. Choose from a good snack menu, which includes sandwiches and baguettes, or go for something more substantial such as roast beef salad, lasagne or steak and mushroom pie. Everything is cooked on the premises and there are various game dishes in season.

④ Turn right at the next main junction and follow the bridle track along the field edge. On the left are glimpses of **Chichester Harbour**, with its complex network of watery channels and sprawling mudflats, distantly visible on a clear day. Pass several ancient burial **tumuli** and then descend through an area of beech woodland. Keep going until you reach the road, turn right and walk through the pleasant village of **Stoughton**.

⑤ Pass the entrance to **St Mary's Church** on the left, followed by the **Hare and Hounds** pub. Continue through the village and on the right is the **Monarch's Way**. Follow the road out of **Stoughton**, all the way to the left-hand bend where you'll see the entrance to the car park on **Stoughton Down** on the right, where the walk began.

Arlington's Lakeside Trail

Combine this delightful walk with a little birdwatching as you explore the banks of a reservoir by the Cuckmere River.

•DISTANCE•	3 miles (4.8km)
•MINIMUM TIME•	1hr 30min
•ASCENT / GRADIENT•	82ft (25m) ▲ ⛰ ⛰
•LEVEL OF DIFFICULTY•	🚶 🚶 🚶
•PATHS•	Field paths and trail, some brief road walking, 13 stiles
•LANDSCAPE•	Level lakeside terrain and gentle farmland
•SUGGESTED MAP•	aqua3 OS Explorer 123 South Down Ways – Newhaven to Eastbourne
•START / FINISH•	Grid reference: TQ 528074
•DOG FRIENDLINESS•	Mostly on lead – as requested by signs en route
•PARKING•	Arlington Reservoir
•PUBLIC TOILETS•	At car park

BACKGROUND TO THE WALK

It was in 1971 that Arlington's rural landscape changed in both character and identity. A new reservoir was opened, supplying water to the nearby communities of Eastbourne, Hailsham, Polegate and Heathfield. Study the blurb on the grassy bank and you'll learn that the area of the reservoir is equivalent to 121 football pitches and that the maxium depth of the lake is 37ft (11.3m), deep enough to submerge four single decker buses.

Fishing

The 120-acre (46ha) reservoir was formed by cleverly cutting off a meander in the Cuckmere River and it's now an established site for wintering wildfowl, as well as home to a successful rainbow trout fishery. Besides the trout, bream, perch, roach and eels make up Arlington's underwater population. Fly fishing is a popular activity here and the lake draws anglers from all over Sussex.

The local nature reserve was originally planted with more than 30,000 native trees, including oak, birch, wild cherry, hazel and hawthorn. The grassland areas along the shoreline are intentionally left uncut to enable many kinds of moth and butterfly to thrive in their natural habitats. Orchids grow here too.

Bird Watching

Arlington Reservoir, a designated Site of Special Scientific Interest (SSSI), is a favourite haunt of many birds on spring and autumn migrations and up to 10,000 wildfowl spend their winter here, including large numbers of mallard and wigeon. The shoveler duck is also a frequent visitor and most common as a bird of passage. You can identify the head of the shoveler drake by its dark, bottle-green colouring and broad bill. The breast is white and the underparts bright chestnut, while its brown and black back has a noticeable blue sheen. The female duck is mottled brown.

Great crested grebes, Canada geese and nightingales are also known to inhabit the reservoir area, making Arlington a popular destination for ornithologists. See if you can spot the blue flash of a kingfisher on the water, its colouring so distinctive it would be hard to confuse it with any other bird. It's also known for its piercing whistles as it swoops low over the water. The reservoir and its environs are also home to fallow deer and foxes, so keep a sharp look-out as you walk around the lake.

The walk begins in the main car park by the reservoir, though initially views of the lake are obscured by undergrowth and a curtain of trees. Be patient. After visiting the village of Arlington, where there is a welcome pub, the return leg is directly beside the water, providing a constantly changing scenic backdrop to round off the walk.

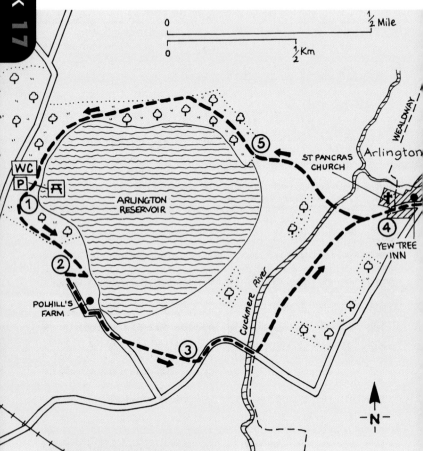

Walk 17 **Directions**

① From the car park walk towards the information boards and then turn right to join the waymarked bridleway. Cut through the trees to a tarmac lane and look for a bridleway sign. Follow the lane and soon the reservoir edges into view again. On reaching a gate signed 'No entry – farm access only' bear right and follow the bridleway and footpath signs.

② Skirt the buildings of **Polhill's Farm** and return to the tarmac lane. Turn right and walk along to a kissing gate and a '**circular walk**'

FOR BIRDWATCHERS

To see the greatest number and variety of birds at Arlington, a visit between October and March is probably recommended. However, for the chance of something unusual, spring and autumn are the seasons to visit. Fresh water acts like a magnet for migrant species and the chance of discovering a garganey, black tern or wood sandpiper is what excites many visiting birdwatchers.

sign. Ignore the gate and keep on the lane. Continue for about 100yds (91m) and then branch left over a stile into a field. Swing half right and look for a second stile to the right of a pond. Cross a third stile and go across a pasture to a fourth.

WHERE TO EAT AND DRINK

Arlington Reservoir has a **picnic site** by the car park where you can relax before or after the walk. The **Yew Tree Inn** at Arlington has a children's play area, beer garden and a choice of home-cooked dishes. Lunch and dinner are served every day and there is a choice of real ales. Nearby is the **Old Oak Inn,** originally the village almshouse and dating from 1733. The likes of Newhaven cod in batter, curry and steak-and-kidney pudding feature on the menu.

③ Turn left and follow the road as it bends right. Cross the **Cuckmere River** and then bear left to join the **Wealdway**, following the sign for **Arlington**. Walk along the drive and when it curves to the right, by some houses, veer left over a stile. The spire of **Arlington church** can be seen now. Continue ahead when you reach the right-hand fence corner, following the waymark. Cross several stiles and a footbridge. Keep to the right of the church, cross another stile and pass the **Old School** on the right.

④ Walk along the lane to the **Yew Tree Inn**, then retrace your steps to the church and cross the field to the footbridge. Turn right immediately beyond it to a stile in the field corner. Cross the pasture to the obvious footbridge and continue to a second footbridge where there are two stiles. Head across the field towards a line of trees, following the vague outline of a path. The reservoir's embankment is clearly defined on the left, as you begin a gentle ascent.

WHAT TO LOOK FOR

Call into Arlington's **St Pancras Church.** One of the most interesting churches in Sussex, it's built of flint and the nave dates back to Saxon times. Look closely and you can see that there are many examples of different architectural styles. Buy a copy of the guide to the church to enable you to learn more about this fascinating place of worship.

⑤ Cross a stile by a galvanised gate and go through a kissing gate on the immediate right. Follow the path alongside the lake and pass a bird hide on the left. Turn left further on and keep to the bridleway as it reveals glimpses of the lake through the trees. Veer left at the fork and follow the path alongside the **reservoir**.

WHILE YOU'RE THERE

Stop off at the **Arlington bird hide**, opened in 1996, and see if you can identify members of Arlington's feathered population. In spring you might spot an osprey, a large bird which occasionally visits lakes, fens and estuaries and preys almost exclusively on fish. Look out too for house martins, sand martins, sandpipers, blackcaps, kestrels, mallards and dunlins – among other birds. If you are interested in ornithology, a visit to the bird hide is a must.

Happy Valley and Chaldon's Lucky Escape

The aptly-named Happy Valley leads you through heavenly countryside – to a vision of hell!

•DISTANCE•	3 miles (5km)
•MINIMUM TIME•	1hr 30min
•ASCENT / GRADIENT•	246ft (75m) ▲ ▲ ▲
•LEVEL OF DIFFICULTY•	🚶 🚶 🚶
•PATHS•	Well maintained and signposted paths, 7 stiles
•LANDSCAPE•	Downland and flower-rich grassland on Greater London's doorstep, some sections of woodland and working farmland
•SUGGESTED MAP•	aqua3 OS Explorer 146 Dorking, Box Hill & Reigate
•START / FINISH•	Grid reference: TQ 301571
•DOG FRIENDLINESS•	Some short sections where dogs must be on lead, there may be grazing animals at times
•PARKING•	Car park on Farthing Downs, open dawn till dusk
•PUBLIC TOILETS•	Godstone

BACKGROUND TO THE WALK

Nearly everything about this walk is surprising. The map shows a small triangle of countryside, gripped between the fingers of London's suburban sprawl and cut short by the M25 motorway. Yet, as you leave the wide horizons of Farthing Downs and amble through the peaceful hay meadows of the Happy Valley towards Chaldon, you could be a hundred miles from the capital.

If the countryside was lucky to escape development, your destination is even more remarkable. Inside Chaldon Church, the earliest known English wall painting was rediscovered under a layer of whitewash some seven centuries after it was created. Your walk begins in a stunning area of chalk downland, right on the Surrey border. Ironically, it was the Corporation of London that saved Farthing Downs from the expansion of London itself. Long before the Green Belt, the Corporation began protecting open spaces around the capital, and has owned and managed Farthing Downs since 1883.

The Celts were growing crops on these downs by the time of Christ, but they quickly exhausted the thin soil and, by Saxon times, the area was being used for burials. When the winter sun shines low over the short grass, you should be able to make out some of the low banks marking the Celtic field boundaries, as well as the circular mounds covering the Saxon graves.

Whitewashed Mural

The graves in Chaldon churchyard are more recent, but the building itself also dates from Saxon times and was mentioned in the Charter of Frithwald in the year 727. So the church was already old by the close of the 12th century, when a travelling artist monk created its greatest treasure – the terracotta and cream mural of the Last Judgement that covers most of the west wall. Heaven and hell are divided by a horizontal layer of cloud. A ladder links the two scenes, and fortunate souls climb towards eternal bliss, whilst the damned tumble off into the flames below. You can read the full story of this grotesque and complex vision in a leaflet in the church, but the wonder is that the painting survives at all.

Sometime around the 17th century the mural was whitewashed over, and it was only rediscovered during the redecoration in 1869 thanks to a sharp-eyed parish priest. When the Revd Henry Shepherd spotted some traces of colour on the wall he stopped the work, and arranged for the painting to be cleaned and preserved by the Surrey Archaeological Society. The mural has recently been cleaned again, following a thorough overhaul of the church itself. Look closely, and you should be able to spot the tiny corner that was left untouched, just to show the improvement.

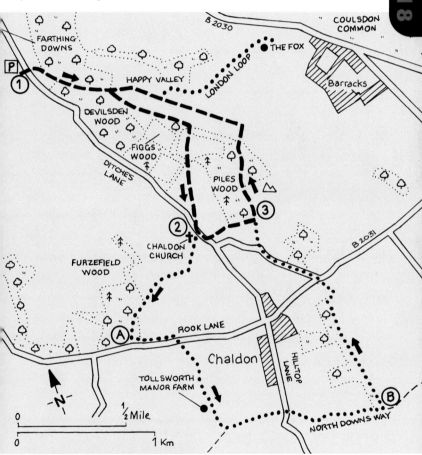

① Cross **Downs Road** from the car park, turn right at the information pagoda, and follow the waymarked **London Loop** down through **Devilsden Wood**. Beyond the woods, the **Happy Valley** opens up in front of you. Follow the woodland edge on your right until the path bears slightly left and begins to lose height. Now dodge briefly into the woods, and follow the signposted path towards **Chaldon Church**. Soon you'll be back in the open, and you follow the woodland edge as far as a wooden footpath sign. Turn right here, and walk through the thin finger of **Figgs Wood** before crossing a large open field.

WHAT TO LOOK FOR ⓘ

You'll hear the continuous, liquid song of the **skylark**, long before you spot the scarcely visible speck that betrays its presence hundreds of feet above the grasslands of Farthing Down. But it's worth scanning the skies for this classic 'small brown job' because, after several minutes, you'll see it plummet to earth in a death-defying dive. Skylarks are ground nesting birds, and the female lays three or four eggs in a cup shaped grass nest that's often barely concealed. In winter, the resident population is boosted by large numbers of migrants from continental Europe.

WHILE YOU'RE THERE ⓘ

There's always something new to see at Caterham's lively little **East Surrey Museum**, which regularly changes its displays of bygones from this corner of the county. Be prepared to encounter anything from local fossils and prehistoric flint tools to medieval pottery and Victoriana. There's also a room with special displays for children, with lots of things for them to see and touch. The museum is open on Wednesdays and Saturdays as well as Sunday afternoons, and has a gift shop, refreshments and toilets.

② At the far side of the field, turn left onto **Ditches Lane**; then, after 40yds (37m), fork right at the triangle to visit **Chaldon Church**. Return via the triangle to **Ditches Lane**, and continue for a few more paces in the direction you were going earlier. Now, you need to turn left onto the public footpath to **Piles Wood**. Cross the open field, and keep straight on when you come to the corner of **Piles Wood**.

WHERE TO EAT AND DRINK ⓘ

The Fox is a large London 'country pub', with stone flagged floors and log fires in winter. It gets very busy but serves pretty good food from a menu of hot and cold bar fare. Families are welcome but dogs only in the garden. The tea room which used to be at the start of this walk, and is still shown on some maps, has now closed, but there is a small refreshment caravan selling tea, coffee snacks and ice creams most weekends and all week during the school summer holidays.

At the far side of the woods you'll come to a gravelled bridleway, where you turn left.

③ Follow the waymarked route of the **Downlands Circular Walk** as it drops down through **Piles Wood** to a footpath cross roads. Turn left, towards **Farthing Downs**, and continue for 700yds (640m) along the bottom of the **Happy Valley**. Should you feel thirsty, you can take the signposted route to **The Fox** that crosses the valley at this point. Turn right, and follow the London Loop waymarks to **Coulsdon Common**. The round trip to the pub will add a mile (1.6km) to your walk. Otherwise, continue for a further 70yds (64m), then fork left and climb gently up the side of the valley to rejoin your outward route at the corner of **Devilsden Wood**.

FOR BIRDWATCHERS 🐦

Although the range of countryside birds seen on this walk may not in itself be striking, the fact they occur so close to London is. Woodland species such as great spotted woodpecker, nuthatch, jay, treecreeper and chaffinch are regularly encountered year-round. In the hedgerows, look out for parties of long-tailed tits and, in winter, flocks of fieldfares and redwings too.

A North Downs Loop at Chaldon

The North Downs Way anchors this route to the national network, and there are some good views towards the Surrey border.
See map and information panel for Walk 18

•DISTANCE•	5½ miles (9km)
•MINIMUM TIME•	2hrs
•ASCENT / GRADIENT•	361ft (110m) ▲ ▲ ▲
•LEVEL OF DIFFICULTY•	🚶🚶 🚶🚶 🚶🚶

Walk 19 Directions
(See Walk 18 map)

You can extend your walk in the Happy Valley by joining a section of the North Downs Way National Trail, a long-distance footpath.

Follow Walk 18 as far as **Chaldon Church**. Pass the church and, as the road swings right to **Court Farm**, nip over the stile and take the path towards **Alderstead Heath**. The path crosses three fields then a stile into **Furzefield Wood**.

Fork left 20yds (18m) beyond the stile onto a concrete path, one of several that were built during the Second World War when this area was being used as a food store. Just before you get to **Rook Lane**, Point Ⓐ, turn left again onto the field-edge path running parallel with the road, and follow it as far as the wicket gate on the right.

Follow the waymarked **Downlands Circular Walk** across **Rook Lane**, onto the concrete drive towards **Tollsworth Manor Farm**. Pass the pretty farmhouse.

Stay with the **Downlands Circular Walk** as it dodges left and right off the concrete road, and follow it down the side of an open field. At the end of the field, the M23/M25 junction rises above the horizon at a gap in the hedge; turn left here, and join the **North Downs Way**. Cross **Hilltop Lane** and, after 750yds (686m), turn left off the **North Downs Way** onto the footpath signposted towards **Rook Lane**, Point Ⓑ. Cross **Rook Lane** at the stile, and keep straight on into **Doctor's Lane**. Just past the pillar box, fork right into **Leazes Avenue**; then, 120yds (110m) further on, fork left at the little green, signposted towards the **Happy Valley**. A few paces further on, you rejoin Walk 18 at Point ③ to return to the car park.

FOR BIRDWATCHERS

Almost unknown in the area until recently, the occasional common buzzard has been observed in the area. So keep your eyes on the skies above as well as on the downland scrub: during spring and summer, blackcaps, whitethroats and lesser whitethroats all appear although their skulking behaviour usually means they are easier to hear than to see.

A Pilgrimage to Waverley

By the enchanting ruins of Waverley Abbey in the Wey Valley.

•DISTANCE•	3 miles (4.8km)
•MINIMUM TIME•	1hr
•ASCENT / GRADIENT•	164ft (50m)
•LEVEL OF DIFFICULTY•	
•PATHS•	Sandy and easy to follow, two sections on minor roads
•LANDSCAPE•	Gently rolling, well-wooded countryside
•SUGGESTED MAP•	aqua3 OS Explorer 145 Guildford & Farnham
•START / FINISH•	Grid reference: SU 870455
•DOG FRIENDLINESS•	Generally good, but dogs must be on lead along roads
•PARKING•	Waverley Lane between Farnham and Elstead
•PUBLIC TOILETS•	None on route

BACKGROUND TO THE WALK

The glory of this walk lies right at the start, just a stone's throw across the fields from the car park. For over 400 years Waverley Abbey stood in this peaceful loop of the northern River Wey and, from here, its abbots wielded enormous religious and political influence. It all began in 1128 when William Gifford, the Bishop of Winchester, founded Waverley on 60 acres (24ha) of farmland. This was the first Cistercian abbey in England, and the original community of 12 monks came with Abbot John from L'Aumone in France. They lived an austere life, devoted to hard manual labour and unceasing prayer.

Spreading the Word

Construction started at once, although it was another 150 years before the abbey church was finally completed. Meanwhile the Cistercians expanded rapidly throughout Britain, and by 1132 there were great abbeys at Tintern, Fountains and Rievaulx. Waverley itself was the springboard for 13 new monasteries; in each case, an abbot and 12 monks, representing Christ and his 12 disciples, went forward as the nucleus of the new community.

At Waverley, as elsewhere, the monks had a significant impact on the local economy as they converted the surrounding forests into grazing and arable fields. They began Surrey's wool industry, and extended their hospitality from the humblest to the greatest. The lavish scale of monastic entertaining seems positively decadent, but these were exceptions to the harsh, everyday routine. Monks rose at 2AM for Matins, spending their time in meditation, study, and manual work before retiring as early as 5:30PM in winter. The day was punctuated by eight services, and by the midday meal of vegetables, bread and beer.

The monks ate in silence in the refectory, accompanied by readings from scripture. You'll see the remains of this building with its 13th-century vaulting during your visit; look, too, for the walls of the Chapter House, where the Abbot presided over the daily business meeting. Of the church itself, only the ground plan and some sections of the chancel walls remain to give you an idea of the scale of the building. The monastic community continued until it was suppressed by Henry VIII in 1536. The estate subsequently changed hands many times; over the years, the buildings were quarried for stone, and many wagon loads found their way into the construction of nearby Loseley House.

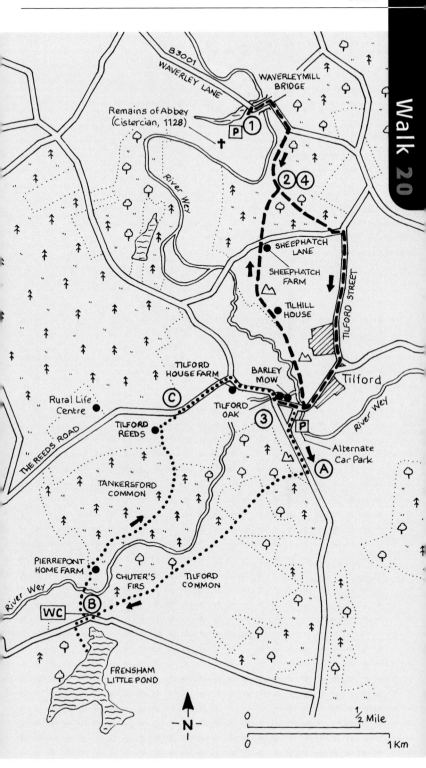

Walk 20 **Directions**

① Turn right out of the car park, taking care to watch out for traffic, and follow **Waverley Lane** (B3001) as it zig-zags left and right over **Waverleymill Bridge**. Continue for 200yds (183m) until the road bears to the left. Turn right here, onto the public byway, and follow it through to a metal gate and public byway signpost.

WHERE TO EAT AND DRINK ⓘ

Half way round your walk, relax in the whitewashed **Barley Mow**, delightfully situated overlooking Tilford's village green. There's cricket here in the summer – but you'll find a good choice of bar snacks and restaurant meals (except Sunday and Monday evenings).

---

② Keep straight ahead and follow the path past **Friars Way Cottage** until you come to **Sheephatch Lane**. Turn left briefly, then right at the junction with **Tilford Street**; there's no pavement for the first 400yds (366m), so go carefully. Now follow the road past the school, over the River Wey bridge and onto **Tilford village green**, where you'll find the **Tilford Oak** and welcome refreshment at the **Barley Mow**.

③ To continue your walk, retrace your steps across the river bridge. Almost at once, turn left at the public bridleway sign just before the **Post Office**. The path climbs gently for 500yds (457m) and brings you to a tarmac lane. Turn left, pass **Tilhill House**, and continue up the narrow sandy track straight ahead. At the top of the short slope, fork right at the public bridleway waymark for the 400yds (366m)

FOR BIRDWATCHERS

As you pass the River Wey, look out for the occasional little grebe or kingfisher (these could be seen in any month) or small groups of ducks (more likely in winter). From October to March, flocks of redwings and fieldfares - sometimes sizeable - may visit the fields, their presence upsetting the status quo for the resident mistle thrushes.

---

climb to **Sheephatch Farm**. Cross **Sheephatch Lane**, where a public byway sign points your way up the gravelled track directly opposite. The track leads you confidently through **Sheephatch Copse**, and soon you'll be dropping down through an ancient sunken way to rejoin your outward track at a metal gate and public byway signpost.

WHAT TO LOOK FOR ⓘ

Beside the green at Tilford, close to the Farnham road bridge, the **Tilford Oak** is said to be at least 800 years old. William Cobbett thought it the finest tree that he ever saw in his life, but now its branches have been lopped and the trunk is patched with iron sheets. In 1822, Cobbett claims that the tree was a full 30ft (10m) round, but his legendary enthusiasm may have run away with him. When the writer Eric Parker measured it in July 1907, its circumference was 24ft 9in (7.5m); he returned in 1934, and found it exactly 1ft (30cm) more. Just opposite this mighty specimen stands a mere sapling, planted in 1902 to commemorate Edward VII's coronation. At the opposite end of the green, its neighbour dates from Queen Victoria's Jubilee in 1897.

---

④ Turn left here for the easy walk back to **Waverley Lane** (B3001). Watch out for the traffic as you turn left, then retrace your outward route over **Waverleymill Bridge** and back to the car park.

A Frensham Loop

Enjoy this extension to Walk 20 by starting from Tilford village green.
See map and information panel for Walk 20

•DISTANCE•	3 miles (4.8km) (this loop only)
•MINIMUM TIME•	1hr 30min
•ASCENT / GRADIENT•	295ft (90m) ▲ ▲ ▲
•LEVEL OF DIFFICULTY•	🚶🚶 🚶🚶 🚶
•DOG FRIENDLINESS•	Not allowed on beaches around Frensham Pond, must be on lead through Pierrepont Home Farm

Walk 21 Directions (See Walk 20 map)

Leave the main route at Point ③ and walk up the left hand side of the green, passing the little car park on your left. Turn left at the top, signposted towards **Thursley and Hindhead**, and continue to the byway crossing at the top of the hill (Point Ⓐ).

Turn right onto the byway, fork left at the waymark post 100yds (91m) further on, and follow the track across **Tilford Common**. Cross the little footbridge at **Chuter's Firs**, and continue past the toilets on your right (Point Ⓑ).

Carry on across **Priory Lane**, bear left through the car park, and drop down the short slope to **Frensham Little Pond**.

Both the Frensham ponds were created in the Middle Ages, to supply the Bishop of Winchester's Court with fish during their stays at his palace in nearby Farnham. The area is now internationally important for its wildlife, and popular for sailing and fishing. Retrace your steps to Point Ⓑ, and turn left at the toilets onto a bridleway. Cross the **River Wey**, and follow the path as it winds left and right around the mellow brick buildings of **Pierrepont Home Farm**. Leave the farmyard through an old iron gate and, after 30yds (27m), take the left hand fork that plunges into the woodlands of **Tankersford Common**. An easy walk brings you to the secluded hamlet of **Tilford Reeds**, where your path swings right onto a gravelled drive for the final section to the **Reeds Road** (Point Ⓒ). Follow the road to the junction at **Tilford House Farm**, and turn right. There's rather more traffic on this road, so do take care on your way back to **Tilford** village green. Turn left onto the green, and rejoin the main walk at Point ③.

FOR BIRDWATCHERS
Frensham Little Pond is host to good numbers of ducks, especially during the winter months. Pochard and tufted duck are usually common, while sightings of goldeneye and smew are less predictable. At migration times, swallows and martins are a common sight and the occasional black tern, wood sandpiper or garganey livens up the birdwatching scene.

A Circuit at Stodmarsh

This easy circuit of a national nature reserve is ideal for birdwatching.

Walk 22

•DISTANCE•	4 miles (6.4km)
•MINIMUM TIME•	2hrs 15min
•ASCENT / GRADIENT•	Negligible 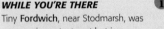
•LEVEL OF DIFFICULTY•	
•PATHS•	Wooden walkways, easy footpaths and lanes, 2 stiles
•LANDSCAPE•	Marshlands, meadows and rustling reed beds
•SUGGESTED MAP•	aqua3 OS Explorer 150 Canterbury & the Isle of Thanet
•START / FINISH•	Grid reference: TR 220609
•DOG FRIENDLINESS•	Dogs aren't allowed on nature trail
•PARKING•	Stodmarsh Nature Reserve car park
•PUBLIC TOILETS•	Stodmarsh and Grove Ferry car parks

Walk 22 **Directions**

This walk takes you through Stodmarsh National Nature Reserve, one of England's most diverse wetland habitats and a place that simply oozes with bird life. Hidden away in the Stour Valley, the reserve has several types of marshland, shallow lagoons and grazing meadows. There are plenty of hides along the way, from where you can get a closer look. Come in the winter and you'll see wildfowl, while in the spring and autumn there are many migratory birds.

Park at the car park near **Stodmarsh** village. An information board tells you what sort of birds to look out for, including marsh harriers, ruffs, siskins and stonechats. Now follow the signs for the nature trail, which at this point leads you through reed beds, a fast disappearing wildlife habitat. It might look as if this is a natural landscape; in fact it is entirely artificial. Early records show that monks from a nearby monastery

once had a stud farm here (hence the name Stodmarsh – the stud in the marsh). They dug ditches in order to encourage flood water from the Stour on to the surrounding meadows where they grazed their horses.

In the 17th century a flood defence barrier, the Lampen Wall, was built by Flemish refugees, allowing them access to the Wantsum marshes and draining the valley. However, when a coal mine opened here, the underground workings caused subsidence and the land became waterlogged. By the 1930s lagoons had appeared and reed beds began to grow. To preserve this habitat and prevent these sites from

> ### WHILE YOU'RE THERE ⓘ
> Tiny **Fordwich**, near Stodmarsh, was once an important port but is now a pleasantly sleepy village. The church, which dates back to Saxon times, houses the mysterious Fordwich stone, once thought to have formed part of a saint's shrine and a possible hiding place for sacred relics. The village's town hall contains the old village ducking stool.

FOR BIRDWATCHERS

In spring, the vast reedbeds are filled with the songs of migrant sedge and reed warblers. But vocal pride of place must go to Stodmarsh's Cetti's warblers – this resident species' explosive song is the loudest of any British songbird. Watch out for birds of prey – marsh harriers are the highlight in spring and summer, with hen harriers featuring in winter.

WHAT TO LOOK FOR

Stodmarsh is a tiny village with an equally tiny village green. There's a sundial on it bearing a verse that states cryptically:

> 'Make time, save time
> While time lasts
> All time is no time
> When time is past'.

Make sense of that if you can.

reverting to scrub, the water levels in the reserve are controlled and the reed beds are managed by harvesting the reeds and grazing the surrounding meadow.

Cross the bridge over the stream, past benches and over another bridge. At the signpost, follow the nature trail again. The route now takes you over two more bridges and along a wide path to a walkway. You might be lucky and see a bearded tit, a pretty little bird that clings to the stems of reeds and makes a distinctive 'pinging' call. Another bird that loves the reeds is the secretive bittern, a relative of the heron, and one of Britain's most threatened species. Cross another bridge and go through a barrier to another path that takes you along the old **Lampen Wall**. Soon reach **Lake Tower Hide**, a large hide on stilts with a great view over the lake.

The path now bears away from the lake and becomes a grassy track. Continue along this for about 1 mile (1.6km), with the **Stour** on your left, until you come to a gate that leads on to the road at **Grove Ferry**. There's a pub here, the **Grove Ferry Inn**, and a pick-up point for boat trips along the river. Turn right and walk down the road, passing signs for a car park and picnic site.

Carry on down the road and turn right at **Elm Tree Farm**. Walk between the farm and the white cottage, go through a kissing gate and continue past another hide and up to a junction of tracks at another kissing gate. Go left here, then cross a bridge over the stream and carry on until you come to another bridge on your left. Cross this and walk diagonally across the field to cross two more bridges. Go through a gate, turn right, walk down the track, pass through another gate and carry straight on. Nip over the second stile on your right, and then make your way over to another stile and walk ahead on to the track. Your way now takes you past **Undertrees Farm** and down to the road. Turn right along the road back into **Stodmarsh**. If you've got time, stop and have a look at the little church. On one of the doors there are crosses made by Crusaders who stopped off to pray on their way to the coast. Turn right in the village and walk back to the car park.

WHERE TO EAT AND DRINK

In Stodmarsh itself, the **Red Lion Inn** offers country cooking and has a garden and a croquet lawn. At Grove Ferry, about half-way round this walk, the **Grove Ferry Inn** serves teas, bar snacks and a good selection of main meals as advertised on a blackboard. In fine weather you can sit outside.

Walk 23

Blean's Ancient Woodlands

A chance to enjoy one of England's oldest woods.

•DISTANCE•	5 miles (8km)
•MINIMUM TIME•	2hrs 45min
•ASCENT / GRADIENT•	82ft (50m) ▲ ▲ ▲
•LEVEL OF DIFFICULTY•	🚶 🚶 🚶
•PATHS•	Field and woodland paths, poorly waymarked in places, 11 stiles
•LANDSCAPE•	Farmland and tracts of ancient forest
•SUGGESTED MAP•	aqua3 OS Explorer 150 Canterbury & the Isle of Thanet
•START / FINISH•	Grid reference: TR 136629
•DOG FRIENDLINESS•	Can run free except close to A290 and grazing animals
•PARKING•	Woodland car park at Gypsy Corner
•PUBLIC TOILETS•	None on route

Walk 23 Directions

The ancient forest of Blean once stretched across a vast expanse of countryside to the north of Canterbury. Patches of this woodland still exist, and there are plenty of paths that lead through them. This is just one walk you can follow and it gives you a great chance to observe a wide range of wildlife. Ancient woodland is that which can be traced back to around 1600, when the earliest maps were produced, and contains native trees such as birch, oak, hornbeam and hazel. A good way of identifying an ancient wood is by the presence of certain wild flowers, called indicator species. These plants don't spread easily and aren't found in great numbers in more modern woodlands. They include bluebells, anemones, wild garlic, dogs mercury, woodland orchids, butcher's broom and herb paris.

Start at the **Clowes Wood** car park at **Gypsy Corner**. Walk back along **Hackington Road** for about for about ¼ mile (400m). Do take care as it's a busy road and there is no footpath. Take the second path on the right – a public bridleway. Pass through some woodland and then go on, beside arable fields and under pylons, to **Well Court**. As you approach the farm, turn left at the poly tunnels and then turn right at the static caravan. Continue to follow the track through the farm, past a willow tree and on past new greenhouses on your right. Your way now takes you between arable fields, through a high hedge and on to a junction of paths. Turn left here between high hedges.

Your path eventually joins a metalled cycle track. Follow the smartly fenced paddock on the left, round to the road. Cross **Tyler Hill Road** and make your way round right and left to pass Blean church. The graveyard here is said to contain the unmarked grave of a young child called Agnes Gibbs. She never grew properly and her tiny body became something of a local

Walk 23

curiosity. Queen Victoria's mother heard about her and had the little girl sent to London so she could see her for herself. Agnes was even examined by the Queen's doctor. Sadly she didn't live long and died at the age of two – only 18 inches (46cm) tall. Medical science was still in its infancy, and her father feared that her body might be dug up by grave robbers who often supplied surgeons with bodies to dissect, so, with the help of the vicar, he buried Agnes at night in an unmarked grave.

Continue on the cycle track to a bridge across a stream. Turn right here into a field and follow the trees beside the stream to the corner of the field. Cross the stile and the wooden footbridge. Continue through woodland with the stream on your left. The path soon veers right and slightly uphill into a paddock. Go left through a kissing gate and on into the car park of the **Hare and Hounds** pub on the **A290**. Cross the main road and turn left over the stream, then right where a metal farm gate is set back from the road. Pass through the white gate and then follow the path round the woodland to the left. After 300yds (274m), at the end of the open paddock, turn right and,

with the high hedge to your left, walk down to the corner. Cross a small wooden bridge, nip over a stile and through a small paddock.

Cross another stream and go along the edge of a field, crossing three more stiles before you come on to a concrete farm road. Turn right and immediately go through the wrought iron gates to follow the road back to the **A290**. Cross the road and turn left up the footpath, pass **Tyler Hill Road** and eventually turn right into **Chapel Lane**. Go left immediately after the converted chapel. The narrow path passes between gardens, then goes left at **Badgers' Farm House** into a field. At the end of the field turn right on to a concrete lane, then continue through the gate marked **Butler's Court Farm**. When you come to two stiles, cross the one on the right-hand side eventually to go over a stiled footbridge.

Cross the field ahead, pass to the right of the cottage garden, go over a stile and left into the tarmac lane. Walk along the lane, then fork left opposite **Arbele Farm** into the field. Your way now takes you across two fields and two stiles, before you turn left, back into the lane. Where the lane forks continue on the narrow path between high hedges and towards **Clowes Wood**. The path continues into the wood, with low branches overhead. At a crossing of tracks continue ahead and walk back to the car park.

Bewitched Otmoor – the Forgotten Land

Explore a desolate landscape, perhaps more reminiscent of the East Anglian fens than Oxfordshire.

•DISTANCE•	4 miles (6.4km)
•MINIMUM TIME•	1hr 30min
•ASCENT / GRADIENT•	Negligible
•LEVEL OF DIFFICULTY•	
•PATHS•	Country road, tracks and paths
•LANDSCAPE•	Remote wetland and farmland
•SUGGESTED MAP•	aqua3 OS Explorer 180 Oxford
•START / FINISH•	Grid reference: SP 563157
•DOG FRIENDLINESS•	Under control in vicinity of firing range. On lead on alternative linking paths across Otmoor
•PARKING•	Spaces near church at Charlton-on-Otmoor
•PUBLIC TOILETS•	None on route

BACKGROUND TO THE WALK

A stone's throw to the north of Oxford lies Otmoor, a canvas of fields and hedgerows that seems to have been bypassed by the rest of the county. A curious ghostly stillness pervades this wilderness, inspiring various writers over the years to describe it romantically as 'the forgotten land', 'bewitched Otmoor' and 'sleeping Otmoor cast under a spell of ancient magic.'

An Abandoned Landscape

Some of it is sheltered and here you can savour the rural charm of green lanes and quiet woodland. Now and again there are signs of life too – the rifle range and the seven villages scattered on various elevations overlooking the perimeter of the moor. The residents once used Otmoor's unpromising terrain for grazing cattle and for wildfowling, fishing and collecting fuel. But mostly it is an austere, abandoned landscape over which the passage of time has had little influence.

With its flat fields, ditches and dykes, it is, in places, reminiscent of East Anglia. On a cold winter's day, and even occasionally in high summer, you can sense Otmoor's sinister, sometimes unsettling, atmosphere. At times it is dark and mysterious, at times it exudes an air of calm and tranquillity. Cross Otmoor as a light mist drifts over the meadows and you'll find the image will linger long in the memory.

Alice's Giant Chessboard

If time allows, journey to the village of Beckley, perched 400ft (122m) over the southern edge of Otmoor, and you'll see why Lewis Carroll was supposedly inspired by the view of this primitive 4,000-acre (1,620ha) landscape to write about the giant chessboard in *Alice Through the Looking Glass*. John Buchan, who lived at nearby Elsfield, described Otmoor in great detail in his novel *The Blanket of the Dark*.

Otmoor for Ever

Centuries ago, Otmoor was waterlogged during much of the year. However, by the late 1820s the moor had been drained and enclosed for agricultural use, as a result of the efforts of landowners. But this was met with fierce opposition from the local commoners, leading to serious rioting in the area. The rioters, who for so long had been allowed to graze livestock on the common land of Otmoor, moved in and destroyed new fences, hedges, gates and bridges. But it was a pointless exercise.

Police and troops were drafted in to help tackle the problem and eventually the rioters acknowledged defeat and withdrew. Nearly 50 local villagers were arrested and taken to Oxford, which happened to be staging its annual St Giles' Fair. The crowds sided with the rioters, shouting 'Otmoor for ever'.

Paradise Reprieved

In the 1980s the moor was at the centre of a bitter row once again, when it was under threat from a proposal to build a new motorway extension. After much opposition, the threat was lifted in order to accommodate a rare butterfly whose breeding ground is Otmoor. In fact the whole area is a paradise for birdwatchers and botanists, and there are many species of birds and plants here. Besides the various resident bird species, many more pass through on a fly-line from the Severn to the Wash.

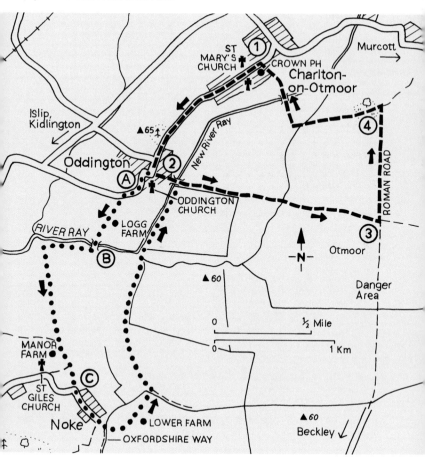

Walk 24

Walk 24 Directions

① Keep the church on the right and walk through the village of **Charlton-on-Otmoor**. Pass **Blacksmiths Lane** and **College Court** and continue on the road. Follow the lane between hedgerows and fields. Soon you reach the sign for Oddington. When the road bends right, branch off to the left by a telephone box, following the sign for Horton-cum-Studley.

FOR BIRDWATCHERS

This fantastic wetland area is a haven for birds and a magnet for birdwatchers. In spring and summer it harbours breeding lapwing, redshank, grasshopper and sedge warblers, reed bunting and many more species. In winter, wildfowl are the main attraction in terms of numbers, with teal and wigeon forming sizeable flocks; in severe weather there is even a chance of finding a party of whooper swans.

② Take the track out of the village, crossing a concrete bridge after a short walk. At the next junction, just beyond it, avoid the galvanised gates on the right, and follow the parallel bridleway, cutting between ditches and hedges. Pass a stile on the left, leading to a linking path which provides an alternative route to the wetlands of Otmoor. The tower of Charlton-on-Otmoor church can be seen at intervals along the track. Continue to the signs for Otmoor's military **firing range**. Keep ahead until you reach a gate on the left and several gates on the right.

③ Turn left at this point and follow the old Roman road north. The track is broad and can be wet in winter. When it curves right, branch off to the left and begin the last leg of the walk.

WHILE YOU'RE THERE ⓘ

St Mary's Church at Charlton-on-Otmoor is a fine medieval building with a tall tower which is a useful landmark when walking on Otmoor. The building is Grade I listed and mentioned in the book *England's 1000 Best Churches* by Simon Jenkins.

④ Follow the path through the trees and soon it broadens to a track cutting between fields and hedgerows. There are good views across a broad expanse of Otmoor to the south. Cross a wooden footbridge and continue on the track. Turn right by some corrugated barns and make for Charlton-on-Otmoor. The church tower is clearly visible now. Cross the **New River Ray** and climb the slope to the junction. Turn left by the **Crown** and return to the church in the centre of the village.

WHERE TO EAT AND DRINK ⓘ

The **Crown** in Charlton-on-Otmoor serves meals and traditional bar food. The only pub on the walk, the Crown benefits from a popular beer garden. Many of the pubs in the nearby villages serve food, including the **Nut Tree Inn** at Murcott, the **Abingdon Arms** at Beckley and the **Red Lion** at Islip.

WHAT TO LOOK FOR ⓘ

There is a **military firing range** on Otmoor. Look for written information about the range at the side of the path and follow the advice carefully. The Emperor moth, marsh fritillary butterflies and Black Hairstreak are among a number of **rare insects** found here. Walk across the moor and you may find the landscape partially puckered with **holes** from World War II bombing practice – a far cry from the serenity of today.

Noke – at the Oak Trees

Make for a sleepy village hidden along the edge of Otmoor.
See map and information panel for Walk 24

•DISTANCE•	8 miles (12.9km)
•MINIMUM TIME•	3hrs
•ASCENT / GRADIENT•	Negligible
•LEVEL OF DIFFICULTY•	🚶🚶 🚶🚶 🚶

Walk 25 Directions
(See Walk 24 map)

Keep ahead on the road through Oddington, following it as it bends sharp right by a telephone box, then round to the left (Point Ⓐ). On the left is **Oddington church**.

Pass the church and continue along the lane. Look for a path, hidden by foliage in summer, beyond the next bend in the road, and go through a dilapidated kissing gate. After several paces, the path reaches the corner of a field. Cut diagonally right across it towards the far corner, making for the end of a line of trees. Keep to the right of **Logg Farm**, join a drive for a few paces, then swing right at the waymark, following a track. As it curves left towards a detached house, go straight on across the field, passing under power lines. Keep the fence on your left. Cross a track to a waymark and keep to the left field boundary, looking for a footbridge in the corner.

Cross the **River Ray** (Point Ⓑ) to a second footbridge and turn right to skirt the field edge. Keep the water on your right and approach a gap in the field boundary. Keep this side of it, turn left and head south, keeping the hedge on your immediate right.

Join a track by a circular tank and keep ahead. Follow the right of way between hedgerows, and veer left at a fork. Where the track curves right towards **Manor Farm**, go straight on along a grassy path left of the outbuildings. Head for a junction with the **Oxfordshire Way** and go straight on to the road (Point Ⓒ).

Keep left, pass **Rectory Cottage** and walk through **Noke** avoiding a path to Woodeaton.

Continue on the lane, passing a sign for **Lower Farm**. Follow the drive towards farm buildings, branching left before them at the fork. Go straight on when you reach a bend. At the next junction, turn left and follow the grassy track, which later narrows to a path. Keep ahead when you reach a clear track and follow it to the next junction by galvanised gates. Turn right and rejoin Walk 24 at Point ②.

FOR BIRDWATCHERS

Outside the breeding season of October to March, the open fields are the haunt of flocks of lapwings, as well as mixed songbird flocks comprising goldfinches, linnets, skylarks and meadow pipits. Predictably, this concentration of potential prey attracts predators so watch out for the occasional merlin, peregrine or short-eared owl.

Enduring Brimpton

A walk through Wasing Park to Brimpton overlooking the Kennet Valley.

•DISTANCE•	6 miles (9.7km)
•MINIMUM TIME•	2hrs 45min
•ASCENT / GRADIENT•	150ft (46m) ▲ ▲ ▲
•LEVEL OF DIFFICULTY•	🚶 🚶 🚶
•PATHS•	Field and woodland paths and tracks, parkland drives, meadow, road and riverside, 11 stiles
•LANDSCAPE•	Common, parkland, woodland and meadow
•SUGGESTED MAP•	aqua3 OS Explorer 159 Reading, Wokingham & Pangbourne
•START / FINISH•	Grid reference: SU 567628
•DOG FRIENDLINESS•	On lead in Wasing Park and Ashford Hill Meadows
•PARKING•	Limited spaces in lay-by opposite Pineapple pub
•PUBLIC TOILETS•	None on route

BACKGROUND TO THE WALK

The English village is one of the key elements that have helped to shape the rural character of this country over the centuries. England's village communities are etched into the fabric of its society, reflecting a way of life that is the envy of others.

Typical Village
However, there has been concern in recent years that some of the time-honoured traditions are being eroded. As we begin the 21st century, so we move into an era of even greater social upheaval. But the village is such a vital and integral part of our rural landscape that, despite the tide of change, it is likely to survive through the next century and beyond – though, almost certainly, in a different form.

Berkshire, like Buckinghamshire, is blessed with many fine villages that, thankfully, have stood the test of time and remained largely intact. Some have fallen victim to planning blight and seen their boundaries expanded in recent years, while others have successfully fought off late 20th-century development, their pride and spirit intact.

One such village that has so far avoided change is Brimpton, just to the south of the A4, between Newbury and Reading. Bounded to the north by the River Kennet and to the south by the lesser-known Enborne, Brimpton, in the main, lies at the end of a breezy ridge. As a village, it's like hundreds of others around the country. But it is that similarity that makes it a typical English rural community. Look closely and you'll see that its key component parts remain in place – the shop and post office, the public house, the primary school and the church are all here.

Village records reveal a fascinating insight into how Brimpton has changed and evolved over the years into the community you see today. As with most rural settlements, Brimpton was once part of the feudal system, shaped and controlled by landowning families, aristocrats and local benefactors. In 1854 the Countess of Falmouth built almshouses for elderly couples and widows, while the Earl donated a small piece of land on which to build a school. Later, when the church was rebuilt, the local squire, James Blyth, objected to the pub being near the church and gave land for a new site.

The local shop was once the home of Duncan McClean, who moved here in 1920. Blinded in the First World War, McClean was a basket and net maker, as well as a poultry farmer. In later years his wife established the village stores. Nearby Glebe Cottage was once known as The Brimpton Refreshment Rooms. Brimpton's villagers, today, are proud of their community. So much so that an illustrated map of the village and its history was unveiled outside the church – marking the new millennium.

Walk 26 Directions

① Follow the path across two stiles to the road. Cross over to join a byway, follow it round to the right and across the **common**. When it swings sharp left, go straight on along the path. Take the path to the right of **Woodside**, bear left at a T-junction and follow the path. Where it joins a track, veer off left

Walk 26

at a waymark, following the field-edge path. Look for an opening in the trees ahead, cross a bridge and turn right at a track, following it to a sign for **Wasing Church**.

② Take the track, turn left at the bend and cut through the wood. Cross a drive to visit the church, return to the drive, turn right and follow it down to the road. Bear left to a junction, then right over the **Enborne** to a fork. Keep left and turn right at the Wasing Estate sign. Veer left along a grassy track to a junction and bear left.

③ Follow the path to the road, turn right for several paces, then left to join the next path. Keep over to the left edge of the field, go through a kissing gate in the top corner and veer right. Turn right to reach a housing estate. Bear right at the road and walk along to the church, following the path beside it. On reaching a field corner, go straight on, swinging left by power lines. Head south to **Hyde End Lane**.

④ Turn left, keeping right at the fork. Look for a stile to the left of a footbridge and cross a meadow. Follow the riverbank to a footbridge and stile. Cross over and take the path to a stile and bridge. Cross the road and follow the track, taking the path to the left of it along the woodland edge and making for a bridge in the far right corner of the

---

FOR BIRDWATCHERS

Common Buzzards are often seen on this walk. Scan the flooded gravel pits at Brimpton for great crested grebe and kingfisher; both species are present year-round. Duck numbers are greatest in winter and at this time flocks of lapwings often feed on the neighbouring fields. Ashford Hill Meadows (a National Nature Reserve) offers a short diversion; here the countryside is so unspoilt that it is like stepping back a century.

---

field. Follow a line of trees to a stile and cross the next pasture towards buildings. Approaching a gate and a cottage, veer left to a stile. Cross to another stile by the road.

⑤ Turn right over the bridge and bear left to a gate leading into **Ashford Hill Meadows**, veering left across pastures. After 75 yds (68m) it becomes enclosed by trees, look closely for a fork and branch off left to a footbridge. Begin crossing a field and after about 120yds (109m), make for a gate on the left. Swing right and keep left at the fork after about 50yds (45m). Look for a stile at the fence corner and follow the path up through the trees. Head for a stile, turn left and cross the field to the next stile. Go straight ahead along a lane and when it bends right, bear left and follow the path to the road. Continue ahead, returning to the lay-by by the inn.

WHAT TO LOOK FOR

Ashford Hill Meadows is a delightful area to explore on foot. The English Nature site is managed by traditional hay cutting and grazing and includes damp meadows, dry grasslands and areas of shrub and woodland. A range of habitats supports an outstanding variety of flowers and insects.

WHERE TO EAT AND DRINK

The **Pineapple**, at the start and finish of the walk, is a picturesque thatched pub. Where the pineapple comes from, no one really knows! Inside are low ceilings, quarry tiled floors, beams and fireplaces, giving it a cosy, intimate feel. The **Three Horseshoes** at Brimpton is a village local. with a choice of snacks and main meals. Alternatively, you might like to wait until you get to the **Ship Inn**, which also has a post office at the rear of the building.

A World of Water and Wildlife at Dinton Pastures

This fascinating walk mostly stays within the boundaries of a popular country park, visiting six different lakes along the way.

•DISTANCE•	3 miles (4.8km)
•MINIMUM TIME•	1hr 30min
•ASCENT / GRADIENT•	Negligible
•LEVEL OF DIFFICULTY•	
•PATHS•	Lakeside and riverside paths, some road walking, no stiles
•LANDSCAPE•	Extensive lakeland
•SUGGESTED MAP•	aqua3 OS Explorer 159 Reading, Wokingham & Pangbourne
•START / FINISH•	Grid reference: SU 784718
•DOG FRIENDLINESS•	Dogs under control and on lead where requested
•PARKING•	Large car park at Dinton Pastures
•PUBLIC TOILETS•	Dinton Pastures

BACKGROUND TO THE WALK

Dinton Pastures Country Park describes itself as a mosaic of rivers, meadows, lakes and woodland. The lakes were once gravel workings that were flooded to form the focal point of this attractive recreational area. Paths and self-guided trails enable visitors to explore this tranquil world of water and wildlife at will and, as you explore the park on foot, spare a thought to work out how it all began.

The Early Days

The park's river meadows were once farmed by Anglo Saxons who called the area Whistley – 'wisc' meaning marshy meadow and 'lei', a wooded glade or clearing. The River Loddon was also used as part of the same process, farmed for its rich supply of eels, caught in willow traps for the monks of Abingdon Abbey. Traps were still in regular use as late as the 1930s.

By the beginning of the 17th century, much of the area formed part of Windsor Forest, where the Monarch and his courtiers indulged in hunting for pleasure. It was the courtiers who built some of the region's grandest houses, including High Chimneys, which was handy for Windsor Castle, the royal powerhouse. High Chimneys' farmhouse, which later became the Tea Cosy café, dates back to 1904. During the mid-1920s it was occupied by a farmer who named the farm after his home village of Dinton, near Aylesbury.

Dinton Pastures forms part of the Loddon's flood plain and is a rich source of gravel, which has been extracted here for more than 100 years. There was an extensive extraction programme here during the late 1960s and right through the 1970s. Much of the material was used to construct the M4 and the A329(M), connecting Reading and Wokingham.

Recreational Area

Comprising about 230 acres (93ha) and officially opened to the public in 1979, Dinton Pastures attracts many visitors who come here to walk, fish, picnic and indulge in birdwatching – a welcome green space on Reading's doorstep. The largest of the lakes at

Dinton Pastures is Black Swan. The Emm Brook once flowed where the lake is now situated. It was later diverted and the oaks which you can see on the island in the lake were once on the banks of the old stream.

All the lakes draw a variety of wetland birds such as swans, geese, coots and moorhens. The park's rarest birds are bitterns – less than 20 pairs breed in Britain annually. Several fly here in winter and in spring migrants such as nightingales also make the journey from Africa to nest at Dinton Pastures. The park offers all sorts of surprises – you may spot a weasel or a stoat, catch sight of a mink in the Loddon, or identify one of 18 species of dragonfly in the lakes and rivers.

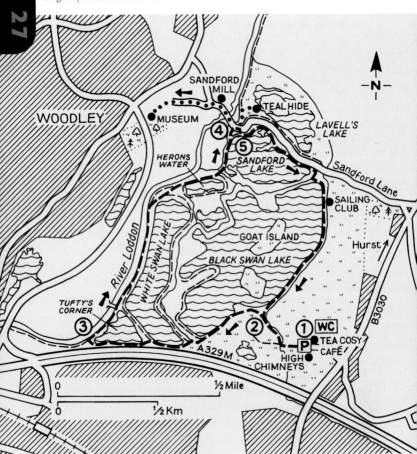

Walk 27 Directions

① With the **Tea Cosy** café and Countryside Service office on the right and **High Chimneys** behind you, cross the car park to the large map of the site. Follow the wide path and keep right at the fork by

the 'wildlife trails' sign. Pass an enclosed play area on the left, keep the **Emm Brook** on the right and enjoy the tantalizing glimpses of **Black Swan Lake** up ahead.

② Swing left on reaching the water and follow the path alongside the lake. When it veers right, turn left

---

WHERE TO EAT AND DRINK ⓘ

The **Tea Cosy** café overlooks a pleasant garden with several tables to enable you to enjoy refreshments outside. It serves cream teas and cakes as well as main meals. If you prefer a pub, try the nearby **Castle Inn** at Hurst, with its historic bowling green, reputedly laid for Charles I. Part of the inn known as the coffin room is said to be haunted!

FOR BIRDWATCHERS

This site boasts ornithological interest throughout the year. In autumn and winter, duck numbers are at their highest; pochard, tufted duck and gadwall predominate but in severe weather, smew and goldeneye sometimes appear. In spring and summer, waterside scrub and reeds are the haunt of reed and sedge warblers, and reed buntings, while great crested grebes float gracefully on the open water.

---

across a bridge to a sign for Tufty's Corner. Bear right here and keep left at the fork after a few paces. Follow the path beside **White Swan Lake** to a waymark post by a patch of grass and a flight of steps. Avoid the steps but take the left-hand path and follow it to the lake known as **Tufty's Corner**. On reaching a junction by a bridge, turn right and keep the **River Loddon** on your left.

③ Walk along to the next bridge. Don't cross it; instead continue on the riverside path. White Swan Lake lies over to the right, glimpsed at intervals between the trees. Further on, the path curves to the right, in line with the river, before reaching a sign 'private fishing – members only'. Join a track on the right here and bear left. Pass alongside **Herons Water** to a sign 'Sandford Lake, Black Swan Lake and Lavell's Lake – Conservation Area'. Turn left and keep **Sandford Lake** on the right. When the path curves right, go out to the road.

④ To visit the **Berkshire Museum of Aviation**, bear left and pass **Sandford Mill**. Take the road signposted 'No Through Road' on the left, pass several cottages and continue ahead when the road dwindles to a path. The museum is on the left. Retrace your steps to Sandford Mill and keep ahead to a footpath and kissing gate on the left. Keep left at the first fork, then right at the second and head for the **Teal hide**. Return to the road, cross over and return to the path.

⑤ Continue with **Sandford Lake** on your right. On reaching a sign 'Sandford Lake – wildlife area – dogs under control' veer left over a bridge and turn left. **Black Swan Sailing Club** can be seen on the left. Continue on the broad path and look out across the lake to **Goat Island**, noted for its population of goats. On reaching the picnic area overlooking **Black Swan Lake**, turn left and retrace your steps back to the main car park.

WHILE YOU'RE THERE ⓘ

Visit the **Teal Hide** at Lavell's Lake, overlooking the wader scrapes. See if you can spot wading birds from here – look out for the green sandpiper and redshank, ducks, swans, kingfishers and the occasional bittern. This site is for serious ornithologists. Not long ago this corner of the park was a meadow grazed by cattle or cut for hay, though the landscape changed dramatically at the time of gravel extraction. Take time to visit the **Berkshire Museum of Aviation**, just off the main route of the walk. The museum is dedicated to the contribution the county has made to flying.

The Canal Reservoirs

Birdlife abounds on the reservoirs of Marsworth and Wilstone.

•DISTANCE•	4½ miles (7.2km)
•MINIMUM TIME•	2hrs
•ASCENT / GRADIENT•	70ft (21m)
•LEVEL OF DIFFICULTY•	
•PATHS•	Tow paths, tracks, some fields, 12 stiles
•LANDSCAPE•	Gentle clayland of Vale of Aylesbury and four great canal reservoirs, now nature reserves
•SUGGESTED MAP•	aqua3 OS Explorer 181 Chiltern Hills North
•START / FINISH•	Grid reference: SP 919140
•DOG FRIENDLINESS•	Lots of birds on reservoirs (plus plenty of other dogs)
•PARKING•	Startops End Reservoir car park, Marsworth, B489
•PUBLIC TOILETS•	None on route

Walk 28 Directions

From the **Startops Reservoir car park** go to the **Grand Union Canal**, to the left of the **Bluebells Tea Room**. Turn left on to the tow path and walk under Bridge 132. At the canal junction go left, signed 'Aylesbury 6¼ miles', on to the Aylesbury Arm. This part of the canal was completed in 1814 and is remarkable for its narrow – 7ft (2.1m), locks. Keep on the tow path, passing six locks, until Bridge 2, known locally as **Dixon's Gap Bridge**. Through the bridge go left over a stile to a footpath alongside a hedge, then along an overgrown green lane into **Wilstone** village.

Wilstone is notorious for Hertfordshire's last witch hunt. A so-called witch, Ruth Osbourn, was murdered here in 1751. After the inquest, held in the Half Moon pub, Thomas Colley, a local chimney-sweep, was hanged at Hertford. Later his body was hung in chains, at nearby Gubblecote.

In Wilstone check out the **Half Moon** pub and **St Cross Church**. Pass the war memorial and continue down the main street. Beyond **Chapel End Lane** and just before the bend go right, through an iron kissing gate and over a stream. Shortly cross a gravel drive, then another footbridge and head diagonally across pasture to a stile. Cross the road, turn left and follow the path alongside the foot of the reservoir embankment. By the **Wilstone car park** climb steps to the embankment. Turn right, so that the reservoir is to your left.

These reservoirs are now nature reserves and are havens for

WHAT TO LOOK FOR

In the evening around Startops and Marsworth Reservoirs you might be lucky enough to see several **Brandts bats** sweeping through the sky. These rare bats were first recorded here in 1975, their first sighting in Hertfordshire. More likely you will see the commoner Noctule and Daubenton bats hunting insects in the twilight.

waterfowl and other birds. You can expect to see tufted ducks, pochard, golden eye, goosander, terns, warblers, buntings, water rail, bitterns, cormorantss, great crested grebes and many others. At various points there are bird hides for you to watch this profusion.

Crossing the bridge at the end of the embankment, the path moves into the tree belt along the west side of the reservoir. Keep straight on across a stream, and climb a stile to cross pasture. This leads to another stile and a footbridge at the head of a reedy inlet. Now in an arable field, the path leaves the reservoir and follows a hedge. It turns left and right to skirt two sides of a field. Ahead is the embankment of the **Wendover Arm branch canal**. Halfway towards it go left by a footpath post, then right to climb to the canal tow path. Over a stile turn left along the tow path – here the canal is dry and its bed is filled with scrub. The **Wendover Arm**, opened in 1797, never held water literally or financially – it leaked like a sieve. A stop lock was finally built at Little Tring in 1904 and this stretch became dry. Follow the tow path as it winds along the 400ft (122m) contour until it curves sharply right. Here climb a stile, go left to a gate, then turn right on to a lane.

Just before some cottages turn left, signposted 'Tringford Pumping Station', along a track. Go left at a signpost (on the right is the pumping station). Over a stile head to a path beneath large horse chestnut trees, to skirt the west side of **Tringford Reservoir**.

Among the many engineering challenges, canal-builders must ensure that enough water is

---

> **FOR BIRDWATCHERS**
>
> The greatest number and variety of birds is found on these reservoirs outside the breeding season, duck populations being particularly high in late winter. During migration times in spring and autumn, watch for passing waders, such as green and common sandpipers, feeding along the shores and for flocks of swallows and sand martins hawking insects over the open water.

available to replenish their locks many times a day. The Tring Summit of the Grand Junction Canal had many locks up from the south and down into the clay vales to the north, all thirsty for water. The answer was to build reservoirs to store water from local streams and wells, then pump it to the canal as needed. The first was dug in 1802 and is now part of the Wilstone Reservoir. In 1806 came the Marsworth Reservoir, Tringford in 1816 and Startops End in 1817.

Emerging from the trees, walk along the embankment to a road. Turn right and at the start of a lay-by car park, cross the road to go sharp left through a kissing gate. The track curves right and emerges from woodland onto the dam between **Marsworth Reservoir** (right) and **Startops End Reservoir** (left). At the canal turn left along the tow path. Where the canal bears right go straight on through a gate to the **car park**.

> **WHERE TO EAT AND DRINK**
>
> At the beginning of the walk at Startops End are two options. The **Bluebells Tea Room** serves food beyond tea and cakes. The **White Lion** (north of the road and opposite the car park entrance) is a typical canalside pub. In Wilstone village there is the **Half Moon** pub and a post office and **general store**.

Places and Palaces in Danbury Country Park

A gentle countryside walk, with panoramic views, exploring ancient woodland, flower-filled meadows and bird-filled lakes.

•DISTANCE•	4 miles (6.4km)
•MINIMUM TIME•	2hrs
•ASCENT / GRADIENT•	164ft (50m)
•LEVEL OF DIFFICULTY•	
•PATHS•	Grass and woodland paths, field paths, some road
•LANDSCAPE•	Ancient woodland, lakes, meadows
•SUGGESTED MAP•	aqua3 OS Explorer 183 Chelmsford & The Rodings, Maldon & Witham
•START / FINISH•	Grid reference: TL 781050
•DOG FRIENDLINESS•	Some open space but must be on lead most of way
•PARKING•	Free car park off Main Road opposite library and inside Danbury Country Park
•PUBLIC TOILETS•	Main Road car park, car parks at Danbury Country Park which also have facilities for disabled

BACKGROUND TO THE WALK

Danbury is surrounded by delightful woodland, much of it common land, and is the largest area of woodland in Essex after Epping Forest. Steep hillocks and heathland soil have prevented intensive arable farming and, as a result, its environs are now designated nature reserves, owned and managed by various conservation agencies, including the National Trust and the Essex Wildlife Trust. These areas pack in a huge variety of habitats in a relatively small space and, if you're a lover of woodland walks, then a stroll around Danbury is bound to appeal.

Diminutive Danbury

The village is perched on a hill, 350ft (107m) above sea level, on the A414 east of Chemsford. The slender spire of St John the Baptist Church is visible for miles around, especially if you're approaching along the A12 from London. This superb setting compensates for what Danbury lacks in historic buildings and, apart from the church, there is little to detain you in the village.

From Place to Palace

On this gentle walk you'll discover some characterful 18th- and 19th-century farms and cottages and the rather splendid 16th-century Danbury Palace, (off limits to the public) inside the country park. Sir Walter Mildmay, founder of Emmanuel College, Cambridge, built the house you see today and called it Danbury Place. But when it was sold to the Church of England in 1845 for £24,700, and occupied by George Murray, 96th Bishop of Rochester, it became known as Danbury Palace, reflecting its change in status.

In the 13th century, aristocratic families went deer hunting in the park, which had been a gift to Geoffrey de Mandeville, 1st Earl of Essex, by William I. Today the country park has three delightful duck-filled lakes, picnic areas and impressive specimens of beech and oak. Beside the palace there are beautiful ornamental gardens filled, in summer, with flowers from Asia and the Americas, while herbaceous perennials attract a host of butterflies.

Your journey's end is at St John the Baptist Church, in a location where Iron Age farmers once lived. Having risen to these comparatively dizzy heights, look southwards where the views are impressive, and you soon understand why the Saxons fortified this position. The Normans, following in their footsteps, built the church and everyone was happy for a time. But, when Henry VIII decreed that the monasteries should be dissolved in 1536, church furnishings were sold to avoid confiscation. The story goes that a medieval DIY enthusiast used much of the wood from the church to kit out the Griffin Inn across the road and, until a few decades ago, part of the rood screen could still be seen above the bar.

Walk 29

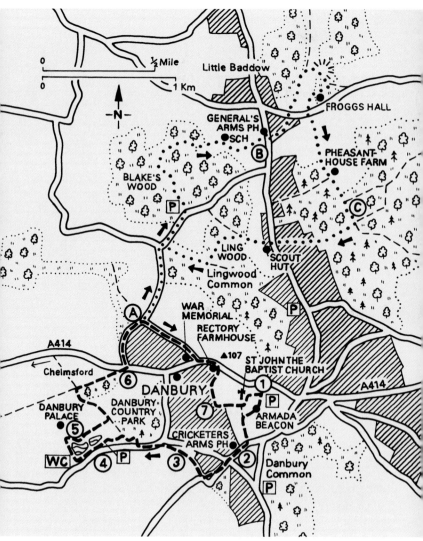

Walk 29 Directions

① Leave the car park via the grassy path to the right of the leisure centre. Walk downhill, with the playing fields left and hedgerows right. One hundred yards (91m) after the **Armada beacon**, turn left at the cross path for panoramic views of south Essex towards Kent.

② Turn right into **Pennyroyal Road** past the Cricketers Arms, then cross **Bicknacre Road** into **Sporehams Lane**. Follow the path marked '**Butts Green**'. At a signpost, take a track through dwarf oaks and gorse, to cross a bridge. After 25yds (23m), turn right, past houses in **Fitzwalter Lane**.

③ At the last house, called **Dane View**, keep left and follow the footpath through woodland to **Woodhill Road**, and turn left to the sign marking the entrance to **Danbury Country Park** on the right. In the car park take the kissing gate on the left and go left again on to the path just before the information board.

④ Maintain direction past another car park and a second lake, until you reach the toilets. Turn right between the lakes, and continue ahead to reach the wall of the **Danbury Conference Centre**.

FOR BIRDWATCHERS

This is an ideal place to become familiar with the range and variety of woodland birdsong in spring. Anytime from March onwards can be good but visit in early May and the songs of migrant visitors such as willow warbler, chiffchaff and blackcap will be competing with those of the resident tits, song thrushes, robins and chaffinches.

WHERE TO EAT AND DRINK

The **Cricketers Arms** makes a good stop for liquid refreshment and also serves a range of bar meals. Try the **Griffin Inn**, just across the road from the church, for great snacks and sandwiches.

⑤ Turn right through formal gardens and, with the lake on your right, follow the path half left through woods. Maintain direction uphill, diagonally across a meadow and through the kissing gate. From the kissing gate, walk half left uphill towards the copse. Follow the boardwalk around the small water-filled gravel pit, then take the path uphill between red-and-white painted posts and continue ahead, passing a yellow waymark. Cross the meadow towards the oak trees, keeping the white metal posts to your right.

⑥ At the last white post, turn left and cross the stile carefully on to the busy **A414**. Cross the road into **Riffhams Lane**, and walk uphill to **Elm Green Lane**. Here turn right, uphill, to the **A414** by the war memorial on the green. Cross the A414, turn left along the verge and right along the footpath beside the **Rectory Farmhouse**.

⑦ At the T-junction turn left for views of St John the Baptist Church and graveyards. At the second T-junction, turn left to visit the church. Turn right to rejoin your outward path past the radio mast and return to the car park.

WHILE YOU'RE THERE

Visit Danbury Palace's 18th-century **Ice House**. Ice was collected from lakes, or imported from Scandinavia and America, and stored here between layers of straw. It was then cut up and popped into summer drinks and desserts.

Danbury Wildlife

A longer loop to encompass the woods and wildlife around Danbury.
See map and information panel for Walk 29

•DISTANCE•	5½ miles (8.8km)
•MINIMUM TIME•	2hrs 30min
•ASCENT / GRADIENT•	148ft (45m) ▲▲▲
•LEVEL OF DIFFICULTY•	🚶🚶🚶

Walk 30 Directions
(See Walk 29 map)

From Point Ⓐ continue along **Riffhams Lane** and, at the junction, bear right into **Riffhams Chase** and left into **Blakes Wood** car park. Take the path to the left of the information board, into a dense area of Blakes Wood dominated by hornbeam and chestnut. Keep the stream to your left.

After 300yds (274m) you reach an area of fallen trees, the result of storm damage in 1987, which the Essex Wildlife Trust have fenced off as an experiment to allow natural regeneration. The path now rises leaving the stream behind, and you emerge into **Colam Lane** passing the school on your left. Follow the footpath into **Parsonage Lane** to meet **The Ridge** with the General's Arms pub on the left, Point Ⓑ.

At **Parsonage Lane** turn right and take the first left into **Mill Lane**. Cross **Spring Elms Lane** and follow the footpath, keeping the white house on your right. Pass the sign for **Heather Hills Nature Reserve** and, at the next fingerpost, turn right past viewpoints across farmland to your left. At the next

fingerpost turn right, passing the brick walls enclosing **Froggs Hall** on your left. Cross a stile, turn immediately left through woodland and, after 200yds (183m), cross **Spring Elms Lane** to pick up the footpath to a bridleway, **Postman's Lane**. Keep the grazing land of Pheasanthouse Farm on your left.

You are now deep in the heart of the **Danbury Ridge**, a 240 acre (97ha) area of long established woodlands. At an information board, Point Ⓒ, turn right into the residential area of **Fir Tree Lane**, cross **The Ridge** and pick up the footpath to the right of the bus stop. Pass the scout hut on your left, and cross the stile into **Lingwood** which used to be grazing land but is now covered with birch and oak. The path continues to **Riffhams Chase** where you turn left into **Riffhams Lane** to rejoin Walk 29.

FOR BIRDWATCHERS
All three British woodpecker species, lesser spotted, great spotted and green, occur here, the first being easiest to locate in late winter when territorial males utter their shrill, piping calls. Watch out for hawfinches too; they are usually associated with hornbeam or beech trees. Despite being large, by finch standards, they are rather unobtrusive and can be difficult to spot.

The Wetland Birds of Barnes

Explore the award-winning London Wetland Centre and join the course of the Oxford and Cambridge Boat Race.

•DISTANCE•	3¾ miles (6km)
•MINIMUM TIME•	1hr 30min
•ASCENT / GRADIENT•	Negligible
•LEVEL OF DIFFICULTY•	
•PATHS•	Riverside tow path, muddy after rain
•LANDSCAPE•	Views across Thames
•SUGGESTED MAP•	aqua3 OS Explorer 161 London South
•START / FINISH•	Grid reference: TQ 227767; Barnes Bridge rail ¾ mile (1.2km) or bus 283 (known as 'the Duck Bus') from Hammersmith tube
•DOG FRIENDLINESS•	London Wetland Centre (LWC) is no-go area for dogs
•PARKING•	At LWC (pay if not visiting)
•PUBLIC TOILETS•	At London Wetland Centre

BACKGROUND TO THE WALK

Rowing boats, like birds, glide gracefully through water and also, like birds, you'll see plenty of them during this easy walk. Barnes has long been associated with the Oxford and Cambridge Boat Race. Indeed, the footbridge, added in 1895, was specifically designed to hold the crowds watching the last stage of the 4⅓ mile (7km) race to Mortlake.

Loads of Birds

The riverside functions rather like a wildlife highway, providing a natural habitat for birds. There are plenty of them to see without having to put a foot inside the London Wetland Centre (LWC) – but to omit it would be to miss out on a very rewarding experience. So why not extend the walk and visit the LWC? There are more than 2 miles (3.2km) of paths and 650yds (594m) of boardwalk to explore once you have paid the admission charge.

Four Reservoirs and a Vision

The mother hen of all bird sanctuaries is the Wildfowl and Wetlands Trust at Slimbridge in Gloucestershire. It was founded by Sir Peter Scott, son of the great explorer, Scott of the Antarctic. One of his father's diaries carries the words: 'teach the boy nature' and this was indeed achieved, for Peter Scott became a renowned painter and naturalist. In recognition of his achievements, a larger-than-life sculpture of him stands on a raised gravel island at the entrance to the LWC, the only inner city wetland reserve in the world.

There are now nine wetland centres in the UK. This one began with four redundant reservoirs owned by Thames Water. They formed a partnership with the housing developer, Berkeley Homes and donated £11 million to help construct the centre. The 105 acre (43ha) project took five years to complete. In 2001 the centre won the British Airways *Tourism for Tomorrow* award.

Once inside, there are three main sections: world wetlands, reserve habitats and waterlife. The first contains captive birds from around the world – North America is accessed via a log cabin complete with authentic furniture. There are information panels too. One of them contradicts the popular belief that swans mate for life. Another tells us about meadowsweet, which is found in damp woods and marshes and used in herbal teas, mead flavouring and even air fresheners.

A Chorus of Facts

Back to birds, and why do they make so much noise? The dawn chorus is their way of telling other birds where they are – 'keep off my patch!' is the message – but it's also to attract a mate. Some birds with colourful plumage find this easy, but others have developed a distinctive song to attract attention, of which the cuckoo is a good example.

Walk 31

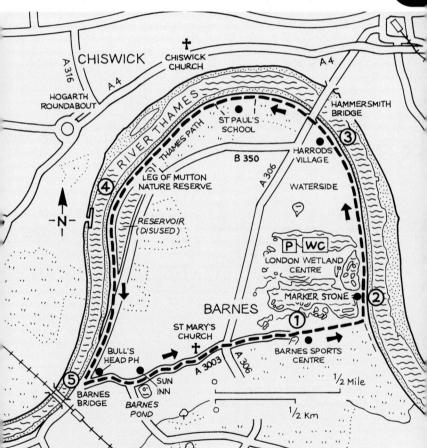

Walk 31 Directions

① Turn left out of the **London Wetland Centre** and follow the path, initially to the left of the

Barnes Sports Centre and then beside some sports fields. At a T-junction turn left along the well-signposted **Thames Path**, alongside the river in the direction of Hammersmith Bridge.

② About 100yds (91m) along the path on the left is a stone post, denoting the 1 mile (1.6km) marker of the Oxford and Cambridge University Boat Race. Steve Fairbairn, who was born in 1862, founded the Head of the River Race and this was the start of the world-famous, annual boat race that traditionally takes place in March.

WHILE YOU'RE THERE ⓘ
Chiswick church could once be reached by a ferry across the Thames, but since 1934 the only way is by bridge. The artist William Hogarth (from whom the Hogarth Roundabout takes its name) is buried in the churchyard. At the rear of the Sun Inn is **Barnes Bowling Club**, where Sir Francis Drake is said to have taught Elizabeth I the game of bowls.

③ The landscaped area of smart flats on the left is called **Waterside** and, a few paces further, a red brick building bears the name Harrods Village. Once past this, as if replicating the trademark Harrods colours of green and gold, is **Hammersmith Bridge**. Follow the path past **St Paul's School**, where *Planets* composer Gustav Holst was a music teacher. On the opposite side of the river, Chiswick Church's green roof is visible.

④ Turn left through a wooden gate into the **Leg of Mutton Nature Reserve**. Continue along the path to the right of this stretch of water, which was once a reservoir. When the path swerves to the left, leave by

FOR BIRDWATCHERS
Although the novelty of seeing birds against a city backdrop is a lure, Barnes is also a genuinely good place for birdwatching. Lapwing, redshank and little ringed plover all breed on a regular basis and there is even a colony of sand martins occupying a man-made bank. Outside the breeding season flocks of ducks are a feature of the site, occasionally panicked into flight by a visiting peregrine.

a wooden gate to the right. Turn left and follow the riverside path towards **Barnes Bridge**.

⑤ Just past the **Bull's Head** pub turn left into **Barnes High Road**. At the next junction, by the little pond, bear left into **Church Road**. Past the **Sun Inn** is a row of village shops and 100yds (91m) further on, the lychgate to **St Mary's Church**. At the traffic lights continue ahead to return to the **London Wetland Centre** and the start of the walk.

WHAT TO LOOK FOR ⓘ
The development, **Waterside**, was constructed by Berkeley Homes after the company purchased 25 acres (10ha) and built the luxury homes that have a unique, bird's eye view of the centre and its wildlife. Adjacent, the **Harrods Village** building was once used to store furniture by those taking up posts in the British Empire. Derelict, it was also sold to Berkeley Homes and it now contains 250 flats with green window frames. Even the security guard wears a Harrods green and gold uniform.

WHERE TO EAT AND DRINK ⓘ
Unlike many on-site cafés, the **Water's Edge Café** at the London Wetland Centre is a delight. It's bright and spacious, serves good quality soups, sandwiches, salads and cakes, and has outdoor seating on large, wooden tables with umbrellas. There are also newspapers to read. The south-facing **Sun Inn** on Church Road, opposite Barnes duck pond lives up to its name – it's quite a suntrap in summer. The usual home-cooked food with a choice of vegetarian options is available here, as is a selection of Tetley's ales and Fuller's London Pride, which is brewed in nearby Chiswick.

Wicken – the Last Survivor

Step back in time through an authentic Cambridgeshire fen, virtually the last of its kind left in Britain.

•DISTANCE•	4¾ miles (7.7km)
•MINIMUM TIME•	2hrs
•ASCENT / GRADIENT•	Negligible
•LEVEL OF DIFFICULTY•	
•PATHS•	Mostly river banks and farm tracks, potentially slippery
•LANDSCAPE•	Low-lying fenland of dykes, scrub and open fields
•SUGGESTED MAP•	aqua3 OS Explorer 226 Ely & Newmarket
•START / FINISH•	Grid reference: TL 564706
•DOG FRIENDLINESS•	Under close control owing to livestock and nesting wildlife
•PARKING•	Wicken Fen nature reserve car park if visiting the reserve, otherwise off Wicken High Street
•PUBLIC TOILETS•	At nature reserve car park

BACKGROUND TO THE WALK

Wicken Fen is one of the oldest nature reserves in the country and, as the last surviving remnant of original fenland left in Britain, one of the most important, too. Over the last 400 years over 99 per cent of East Anglia's ancient Great Fen has been drained and converted into farmland, richly productive for agriculture but largely sterile for wildlife.

Not surprisingly the National Trust's 1,330 acres (539ha) at Wicken have assumed a critical importance. Since they purchased their first tiny piece of land here in 1899, the Trust has made 56 separate acquisitions at Wicken, and the plan is to continue to add to their holdings by acquiring farmland to the south of the reserve and restoring it to its original wetland state. The latest was in October 2001 when the Trust bought 415 acres (168ha) at Burwell Fen Farm for £1.7m, and a display at the visitor centre describes the 'Wicken Vision' in more detail.

Wildlife at Wicken

The nature reserve itself includes a short boardwalk (¾ miles/1.2km) and a longer nature trail (2¼ miles/3.6km), while eight hides allow close-up views over the many ponds and ditches which, depending on the time of year, are often teeming with wildlife. For instance, Wicken Fen hosts over 1,000 types of beetle, and visiting coleopterists (that's beetle-lovers to you and me) once included the young Charles Darwin who came here to collect specimens while studying at Cambridge.

As well as 212 species of spider, Wicken Fen also supports nearly 300 different types of plant. In the summer the ponds and pools buzz with dragonflies and damselflies, and are full of yellow and white water lilies, water mint and water violets, plus the greater bladderwort, a carnivorous plant with small yellow flowers and virtually no roots that feasts on small aquatic life forms. Away from the water the uncultivated grassland features early marsh and southern marsh orchids, usually flowering in June, while in the areas of sedge you can find milk parsley and the light purple flowers of the rare marsh pea. A visit to the reserve is a must, and you should allow the bare minimum of an hour to explore.

Managing the Land

An on-going programme of management is essential to maintain the distinctive character of the land. For generations Wicken peat has been cut for burning, and sedge (a grass-like plant that grows on wet ground) has been harvested for thatching. The peat is now untouched, but sedge is still cut every three years in the summer – just as it has been at Wicken ever since 1419.

Meanwhile konig ponies, already used in the Norfolk Broads, have been introduced to Verrall's Fen to stop cleared scrub from reinvading; and ditches are periodically dredged of choking vegetation by a process with the splendid name of 'slubbing'.

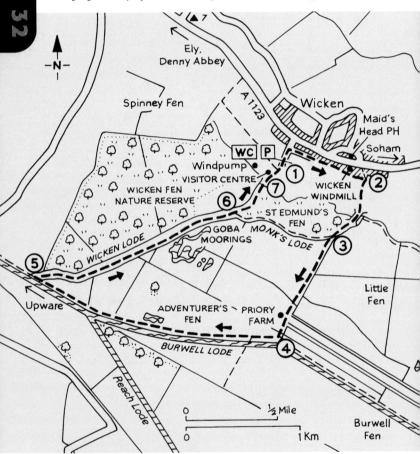

Walk 32 Directions

① From the nature reserve walk up **Lode Lane** towards the village of Wicken. Before you meet the main road turn right on to **Back Lane** and follow this route, behind the houses (including the windmill),

which soon becomes a pleasant track. When you reach the far end of the lane, turn right on to a wide track through the fields. (If you have parked in the centre of the village take the signposted public footpath via **Cross Green**, just along from and opposite the pub, out to the fields.)

WHERE TO EAT AND DRINK ℹ

Ice creams and hot drinks are available at the **visitor centre**, or for a pub meal visit the thatched **Maid's Head** on the green in the centre of Wicken village. Food and drink are also available at the pub in the village of Upware, just off the route, which is situated at the end of Old School Lane and whose full name is apparently **Five Miles from Anywhere Riverside Inn**.

② Follow this wide route down to cross two footbridges. Don't take the path off to the left but continue walking ahead straight on (beyond the green-painted second footbridge) along the bank of **Monk's Lode**, with **St Edmund's Fen** opposite. A lode, incidentally, is another name for an artificially cut waterway.

③ After 550yds (503m) branch left by a newly constructed fence and gate for a long and straight track, known in these parts as a drove, out across the fields to **Priory Farm**. Join the surfaced lane and continue all the way to the end.

④ By the Environment Agency's private raised bridge turn right and walk along the bank of the **Burwell Lode** (don't be tempted by the footbridge). Continue for 1½ miles (2.4km) past **Adventurers' Fen**, named after the 17th-century 'Gentlemen Adventurers' who first started draining the fens in earnest.

⑤ At a high-arched footbridge over **Wicken Lode** turn right and, once over a stile, walk along this bank back towards **Wicken Fen** past a National Trust sign. If you continue across the footbridge and walk for another ¼ mile (400m) you come to **Upware**, with a pub (▶ Where to Eat and Drink) and picnic area.

Ignoring paths off into the open fen and fields on your right, continue along the bank until its junction with **Monk's Lode**.

⑥ Cross the short bridge by **Goba Moorings** and continue alongside **Wicken Lode**, not along Monk's Lode (to the right). The lush vegetation of Wicken Fen is now either side, and across the water you will pass the lofty tower hide, one of several dotted around the reserve.

FOR BIRDWATCHERS

In spring, the reserve is alive with the songs of reed and sedge warblers, blackcaps and reed buntings and you should also listen out for the 'pinging' calls of bearded tits that haunt the reedbeds. Marsh harriers are present in spring and summer, gliding low over the reeds in search of small mammals and birds; in winter, if you see a large raptor it is more likely to be a hen harrier.

⑦ When you get to the end turn left to explore the visitor centre (open Tuesday to Sunday). There is a small admission charge to the reserve itself, which is open daily from dawn to dusk. Near by is the restored **Fen Cottage**, and a lovely thatched boathouse where the reserve's traditional working fen boat is kept. To return to the car park and village, simply walk back up the lane past the houses.

WHILE YOU'RE THERE ℹ

To the west of Wicken (off the A10) is **Denny Abbey**, founded in 1159 by Benedictine monks as a dependent priory to Ely Cathedral. The site is now owned by English Heritage and includes the Farmland Museum, with a traditional farm-worker's cottage, 17th-century stone barn and workshops. It's open daily between April and October.

Fenland's Big Skies

An enigmatic landscape links remote Manea with an historic drainage cut.

•DISTANCE•	6¼ miles (10.1km)
•MINIMUM TIME•	3hrs
•ASCENT / GRADIENT•	Negligible
•LEVEL OF DIFFICULTY•	
•PATHS•	Lanes and hard farm tracks
•LANDSCAPE•	Wide, flat fields separated by ditches and drainage channels
•SUGGESTED MAP•	aqua3 OS Explorer 228 March & Ely
•START / FINISH•	Grid reference: TL 478893
•DOG FRIENDLINESS•	Very good, but no dogs on Ouse Washes Nature Reserve
•PARKING•	Roadside parking in centre of Manea
•PUBLIC TOILETS•	Off Park Road, Manea, and at Ouse Washes Nature Reserve

BACKGROUND TO THE WALK

A landscape that is as flat and bare as the Fens may seem a dull and uninteresting prospect for a walk, but in fact there is much more to this unique place than first meets the eye, and what you see now isn't the way it looked in the distant past. Ancient tree trunks known as bog oaks are periodically uncovered from the peaty soil, proving that this apparently tree-less country once presented a totally different scene.

Until 400 years ago the Fens remained an unwelcoming swampy and impenetrable landscape which local outlaws and tribesmen such as Hereward the Wake, who led his rebels against the invading Normans, could make their own. Small communities such as Manea developed on the pockets of higher ground – the 'ea' suffix is derived from the Anglo-Saxon 'ig' meaning island.

Draining the Fens

Systematic draining did not begin until the 17th century, when the 4th Earl of Bedford turned to Dutch engineer Cornelius Vermuyden to repeat his successful work in the Netherlands. The result was a direct, 20-mile (32km) cut known as the Old Bedford River, which sliced through the lands south and east of Manea taking the winter floodwaters out to the Wash. A rapidly expanding series of drains and dykes followed, gradually turning the ancient bog and swamp into fertile agricultural land, with many of these artificial rivers named after their original width (the New Bedford River is also known as the Hundred Foot Drain, for instance).

But not everyone agreed with the draining of the Fens, however, and there was determined opposition from the 'Fen Tigers', those wildfowlers and marshmen whose livelihoods depended on the traditional Fenland way of life. Even after the drains and dykes became permanent fixtures there were still, until quite recently, occasional throwbacks to another era. When transport and communication proved difficult, particularly for remote communities during the winter floods, the so-called Floating Church would go from hamlet to village providing religious services. The converted barge was still in use into the early years of the 20th century, when it spent two years tied up at Welches Dam, near Manea, which you visit on this walk.

Fenland's Capital that Never Was

An early supporter of the ambitious drainage scheme was King Charles I, who owned 12,000 acres (4,860ha) of wetland surrounding Manea. He backed the enterprise of the early speculators to such an extent that he even took the lead in designing a new capital for the Fens. Complete with a royal palace for himself, it was to be sited near Manea and would be called Charlemont. Alas, he lost his head before the dream was realised.

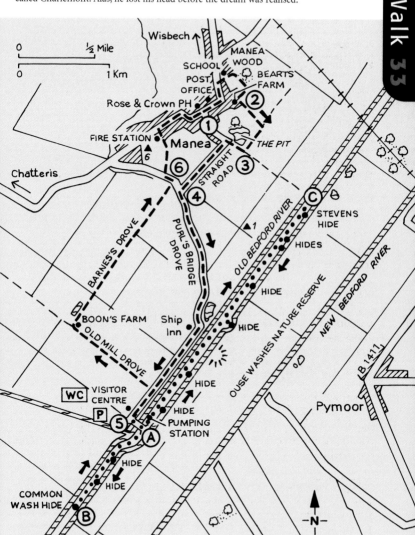

Walk 33 Directions

① Walk eastwards along the **High Street** (which becomes **Station Road**), past the post office and fish and chip shop, then turn right for the public footpath alongside the primary school. At the football pitch at the far end turn right and go past **Manea Wood**, planted in 1997 for the local community with ash, oak, white willow, birch and common alder. Continue along the path as it bears right and approaches **Bearts Farm**.

② Turn left by the old barns and sheds for the wide track out into the fields, with the farm on your

---

WHERE TO EAT AND DRINK ⓘ

The **Rose and Crown** pub on Manea's High Street generally serves food lunchtime and evening, and there's a **fish and chip shop** on Station Road. At the time of writing the **Ship Inn** at Purls Bridge was up for sale and its opening times subject to change. Beer connoisseurs should visit the **Rose and Crown** in nearby March, which has sold over 800 different real ales to date.

---

right, to reach an attractive reedy lake known locally as '**the Pit**'. This was originally dug for clay, which was then transported across the fields on a light railway to shore up the banks of the nearby Old and New Bedford Rivers. The Pit is now a popular place for fishermen and wildlife alike.

③ At the end of the track turn right on to a lane, with the lake still on your right, then when you reach the junction at the corner of the road turn left, on to the appropriately named **Straight Road**, and follow this through the fields to the end.

WHILE YOU'RE THERE ⓘ

The **Wisbech and Fenland Museum** in the centre of Wisbech has a fascinating display exploring the landscape and history of the Fens. The museum, housed in a purpose-built Victorian building with many of its period fixtures and fittings, has other wide-ranging displays and exhibits that include the original manuscript of Charles Dickens's *Great Expectations* and an ivory chess set that once belonged to Louis XIV.

FOR BIRDWATCHERS

The expansive and rather featureless fenland landscape may not be to everyone's taste but there can be no more evocative a setting in which to watch flocks of wintering swans pass overhead. Most activity occurs at dawn and dusk, the birds moving between farmland feeding grounds and wetland roosts. All three British swan species – mute, whooper and Bewick's – occur in good numbers.

---

④ Turn left on to **Purl's Bridge Drove**, signposted 'Welches Dam and RSPB reserve'. Follow this open lane all the way to **Purl's Bridge**, by the **Old Bedford River**. Continue along the bank to reach the **Ouse Washes Nature Reserve**, where there's a visitor centre and public toilets.

⑤ Return along the lane for 440yds (402m) and turn left for the signposted public bridleway by some dark wooden sheds. Known as **Old Mill Drove**, this runs directly across the open fields as far as the rusting farm machinery and outbuildings of **Boon's Farm**. Turn right and walk along the dead-straight **Barnes's Drove** for 1¼ miles (2km) until you reach the road at the far end.

⑥ Turn left and after 80yds (73m) turn off right over a stile for a public footpath across fields back into **Manea** (aim for the fire station tower). The route veers one way then the other as it skirts a series of pig enclosures – just follow the clear yellow waymarks past the enormous porkers which, depending on the conditions, might be wallowing in mud pools. At the far side cross successive stiles and turn right, past the village stores, to follow the main road back to the centre.

Twitching in Ouse Washes

A short hide-by-hide wander along the Ouse Washes Nature Reserve.
See map and information panel for Walk 33

•DISTANCE•	up to 10 miles (16.1km) depending on hides visited
•MINIMUM TIME•	up to 5hrs
•ASCENT / GRADIENT•	Negligible
•LEVEL OF DIFFICULTY•	

Walk 34 Directions
(See Walk 33 map)

The Ouse Washes Nature Reserve is run by the Royal Society for the Protection of Birds (RSPB) and Cambridgeshire Wildlife Trust and, although entrance is free, visitors are requested not to bring dogs. The reserve covers 2,471 acres (1,000ha) of wet grassland that lie in a wide strip almost 20 miles (32 km) long and 1 mile (1.6km) wide between the Old and New Bedford Rivers. Today the area forms the largest area of regularly flooding 'washland' in Britain, and after the flood waters have subsided ducks and waders nest in the fields before cattle are introduced in the summer to keep the grass and sedge short.

In winter, ducks such as pochard, teal and pintail are all regular visitors, plus the likes of migrating Bewick's and whooper swans. Over 53,000 wigeon dropped by during the winter of 1989/90!
Summer has its own attractions, including lapwings and kingfishers, and perhaps the sight of a marsh harrier gliding low over the ground in search of his tea. The network of dykes and pools also supports other wildlife such as dragonflies.

Access to the nature reserve is limited to the bank of the **Old Bedford Barrier**, which defines its western edge.

The ten hides are all free to enter, and binoculars are even available on a hire basis at the visitor centre near Welches Dam, (open daily, 9AM to 5PM). From here cross the bridge by the pumping station (Point **Ⓐ**) and turn right for the hides known as **Welches Dam**, **Rickwood** and **Common Wash** (Point **Ⓑ**), the furthest of which is just under 1 mile (1.6km) distant.

For the more remote and undisturbed hides turn left by the pump house and walk along the bottom of the bank rather than the top (so as not to scare the birds). The furthest is **Stevens Hide** (Point **Ⓒ**), just under 2 miles (3.2km) away.

FOR BIRDWATCHERS

Although winter wildfowl – swans in particular – are the main attraction of the area, the Ouse Washes is fast becoming the place to visit if you want to see barn and short-eared owls feeding during the hours of daylight. Their prey – voles and mice – are concentrated along banks and verges in winter and this is where the owls hunt, often oblivious to the presence of human observers.

Welney's Birds

Stroll along the Summer Walk at Welney Washes to a great bird reserve.

•DISTANCE•	4¼ miles (6.8km)
•MINIMUM TIME•	1hr 30min (allow time for birdwatching)
•ASCENT / GRADIENT•	Negligible
•LEVEL OF DIFFICULTY•	
•PATHS•	Boardwalks and grass paths with benches
•LANDSCAPE•	Reedy wetlands, lagoons and fen
•SUGGESTED MAP•	aqua3 OS Explorer 228 March & Ely
•START / FINISH•	Grid reference: TL 545944
•DOG FRIENDLINESS•	Dogs not permitted
•PARKING•	WWT Welney car park, signposted off A1101
•PUBLIC TOILETS•	At visitor centre near car park
•NOTE•	Summer Walk open in summer only; contact WWT Welney (01353 860711) to check path is open

Walk 35 Directions

The Wildfowl and Wetlands Trust (WWT) reserve at Welney Washes is tucked away in the south east corner of Norfolk, on the border with Cambridgeshire. It covers 850 acres (344ha) of freshwater grazing marshland that floods regularly – the largest such area remaining in Britain. This unique habitat was formed when two massive drainage channels were created, leaving a strip of land between them that is about ½ mile (800m) wide. This area is known as the Ouse Washes.

FOR BIRDWATCHERS

Although restrictions apply to where you can walk in winter, you cannot fail to get spectacular views of the area's Bewick's, whooper and mute swans, and you stand a very good chance of seeing a feeding barn owl during the hours of daylight. In summer, when access is less restricted, look for redshank, lapwing, snipe, grey heron and reed bunting.

The Ouse Washes were not created with the intention of providing breeding areas for birds. Instead, they were designed to act as a reservoir to hold excess water when the main drainage system is unable to cope. Several attempts were made to drain the Fens – by the Romans and by medieval engineers – but it was not until the 17th century that this wilderness of sedge, reed and bog was finally vanquished. The wealthy Duke of Bedford owned a large expanse of fenland, and wanted to do more with it than graze sheep in the summer and watch it flood all winter. He employed a talented Dutch engineer called Cornelius Vermuyden to design a new river system that would allow flood water to be channelled more directly out to sea, rather than flowing into the meandering River Great Ouse.

The cut between Earith in Cambridgeshire and Denver in Norfolk, was named the Old Bedford River and was completed

Walk 35

in 1637. Although it vastly improved the duke's summer grazing grounds, his land still flooded in winter. A second cut was made, running parallel to the first, and called the New Bedford River. The banks on both rivers were raised, so that the area between them could take surplus water during times of flood – the Ouse Washes. When you visit you will see information boards telling you how each river bank has been built up to allow controlled flooding, but to prevent overflowing into the surrounding low-lying land.

WHILE YOU'RE THERE ⓘ

For those who are interested in still more birdwatching, the RSPB has a large reserve at **Ouse Washes**, to the south of Manea at Welches Dam. Facilities include a car park, a visitor centre and several free hides.

Today, the area between the two channels is much as it always was: grazed or cut for hay during the summer and flooded during the winter. Because of this, and because parts are closed during the bird breeding season, this walk is only open for part of the summer – usually July and August – but it's well worth the wait.

This walk takes you through some of the most spectacular birdwatching territories in the country. As visitors are asked not to make a noise or sudden movements that might startle the birds, many species seem totally unaware that they are under scrutiny. A visit to Welney is magical at any time of year, even when the footpath is closed and walkers are restricted to the Screenbank Walk that takes you between hides. Try coming in November, when thousands of

swans crowd into the flooded washes to rest for the night. The noise is spellbinding and white necks poke up like periscopes as far as the eye can see.

Begin at the car park and walk up the ramp to cross the bridge. Go down the steps and turn left. This is called the **Screenbank Walk** and wooden boards shield the Washes to the north from any sudden movements, although there are gaps that allow you to view the wildlife. Soon signs will direct you to the right to the **Reedbed Boardwalk**. This is a taste of what comes later.

When you finish the boardwalk, turn right along the Screenbank Walk until you see a sign to your right for the **Summer Walk**. Follow the waymarkers in a figure-of-eight configuration through reeds and marsh. The route is clearly marked, and easy to follow. Information boards at regular intervals tell you exactly what birds to look for. After completing its loops, the Summer Walk leads back to the Screenbank Walk. Turn left, and retrace your steps to the footbridge.

At the footbridge, continue straight ahead, along the northern part of the Screenbank Walk. Eventually you reach **Buxton Hide**, **Lyle Hide**, **Allport Hide** and **Friends' Hide**, all on your left. This part of the walk is linear, but you will see so many different birds that it won't feel like it. At Friends' Hide, retrace your steps back to the footbridge, cross it, and return to the car park.

WHERE TO EAT AND DRINK ⓘ

There is a little tea room in the **visitor centre** at Welney, where you can sit and read the information about the site. It sells cakes, snacks, teas and coffee.

Blakeney Eye's Magical Marshes

Walk along the sea defences to some of the finest bird reserves in the country.

·DISTANCE·	4½ miles (7.2km)
·MINIMUM TIME·	2hrs
·ASCENT / GRADIENT·	98ft (30m) ▲ ▲ ▲
·LEVEL OF DIFFICULTY·	🚶🚶 🚶🚶 🚶🚶
·PATHS·	Footpaths with some paved lanes, can flood in winter
·LANDSCAPE·	Salt marshes, scrubby meadows and farmland
·SUGGESTED MAP·	aqua3 OS Explorer 251 Norfolk Coast Central
·START / FINISH·	Grid reference: TG 028441
·DOG FRIENDLINESS·	Under control as these are important refuges for birds
·PARKING·	Carnser (pay) car park, on seafront opposite Blakeney Guildhall and Manor Hotel
·PUBLIC TOILETS·	Across road from Carnser car park

BACKGROUND TO THE WALK

Blakeney was a prosperous port in medieval times, but went into decline when its sea channels began to silt up. However, although the merchants decried the slow accumulation of salt marsh and sand bars, birds began to flock here in their thousands. By Victorian times it had become such a favoured spot with feathered migrants that it became known as *the* place to go shooting and collecting. Some sportsmen just wanted to kill the many waterfowl, while others were more interested in trophy collecting – looking for species that were rare or little-known. The maxim 'what's hit is history; what's missed is mystery' was very characteristic of the Victorians' attitude to biological science. Many of these hapless birds ended up stuffed in museums or private collections.

Nature Reserve

After many years of bloody slaughter the National Trust arrived in 1912 and purchased the area from Cley Beach to the tip of the sand and shingle peninsula of Blakeney Point. It became one of the first nature reserves to be safeguarded in Britain. Today it is a fabulous place for a walk, regardless of whether you are interested in ornithology. A bright summer day will show you glittering streams, salt-scented grasses waving gently in the breeze and pretty-sailed yachts bobbing in the distance. By contrast, a wet and windy day in winter will reveal the stark beauty of this place, with the distant roar of white-capped waves pounding the beach, rain-drenched vegetation and a menacing low-hung sky filled with scudding clouds. It really doesn't matter what the weather is like at Blakeney, because a walk here is invigorating in any of its moods.

Although these days we regard the Victorians' wholesale slaughter with distaste, they did leave behind them a legacy of valuable information. It was 19th-century trophy hunters who saw the Pallas' warbler and the yellow-breasted bunting in Britain for the first time – and they were seen at Blakeney. A little later, when the Cley Bird Observatory operated here between 1949 and 1963, the first sub-alpine warbler in Norfolk was captured and ringed.

The Victorians' records tell us that a good many red-spotted bluethroats appeared in September and October, and any collector who happened to visit then was almost certain to bag one. In the 1950s the observatory discovered that these were becoming rare at this time of year. Today, bluethroats are regular spring visitors but are seldom seen in the autumn. It is thought that this change over time is related to different weather patterns and indicates how climate change, even on this small scale, can dramatically effect the behaviour of birds.

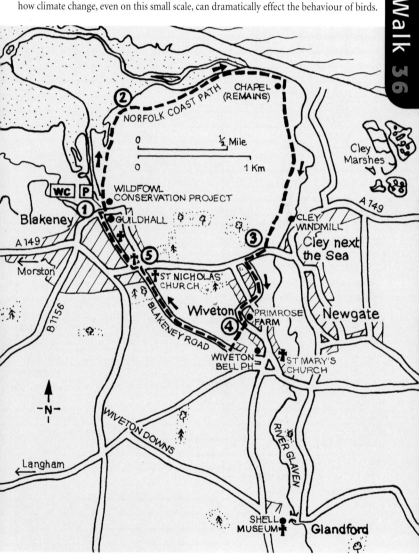

Walk 36 Directions

① From the car park head for the wildfowl conservation project, a fenced-off area teeming with ducks,

geese and widgeon. A species list has been mounted on one side, so you can see how many you can spot. Take the path marked **Norfolk Coast Path** out towards the marshes. This raised bank is part of the sea defences, and is managed by the Environment Agency. Eventually, you have salt marshes on both sides.

② At the turning, head east. Carmelite friars once lived around here, although there is little to see of their chapel, the remains of which are located just after you turn by the wooden staithe (landing stage) to head south again. This part of the walk is excellent for spotting and terns in late summer. Also, look for godwits, turnstones and curlews. The path leads you past **Cley Windmill,** built in 1810 and which last operated in 1919. It is open to visitors and you can climb to the top to enjoy the view across the marshes. Follow signs for the Norfolk Coast Path until you reach the **A149**.

> **WHERE TO EAT AND DRINK** ℹ
> In Blakeney the **Kabin** sandwich bar in the car park operates between Easter and October, and sells snacks, tea and coffee. The **Blakeney Hotel**, **Manor Hotel**, **White Horse** and **King's Arms** all have restaurants and bar food. There are also several shops for picnic supplies. The **Moorings Bistro** serves tea and coffee as well as meals. On the walk itself you can try the **Wiveton Bell**.

③ Cross the A149 to the pavement opposite, then turn right. Take the first left after crossing the little creek. Eventually you reach the cobblestone houses of **Wiveton** and a crossroads; go straight ahead.

④ Take the grassy track opposite **Primrose Farm**, and walk along it until you reach a T-junction. This is the **Blakeney Road**, and you turn right along it. However, if you want refreshments before the homeward

> **FOR BIRDWATCHERS** 🐦
> Walk along the coast and you cannot fail to notice Blakeney's birdlife – there are birds simply everywhere you look. In summer, black-headed gulls and Sandwich, little and common terns are the most conspicuous species. With their evocative calls, brent geese take centre stage in winter as flocks fly overhead or feed out on the saltmarsh.

stretch, turn left and walk a short way to the **Wiveton Bell**. The lane is wide and ahead you will see St Nicholas' Church nestling among trees. This dates from the 13th century, but was extended in the 14th. Its two towers served as navigation beacons for sailors, and the narrower, east one is floodlit at night.

⑤ At the **A149** there are two lanes opposite you. Take the **High Street** fork on the left to walk through the centre of **Blakeney** village. Many cottages are owned by the Blakeney Neighbourhood Housing Society, which rents homes to those locals unable to buy their own. Don't miss the 14th-century Guildhall undercroft at the bottom of Mariner's Hill. Then continue straight ahead into the car park.

> **WHILE YOU'RE THERE** ℹ
> **Langham Glass** at nearby Morston has restored 18th-century workshops, demonstrations and a shop. **Morston Marshes** are in the care of the National Trust and are an important site for migrating wrynecks, icterine and barred warblers. If you have time, a boat trip out to see the seals is a rewarding experience. These endearing creatures breed and bask on the isolated sandbars to the north.

The Ghosts of Dunwich

Conjure up visions of a lost city as you stand on the cliffs gazing out to sea.

·DISTANCE·	8 miles (12.9km)
·MINIMUM TIME·	4hrs
·ASCENT / GRADIENT·	262ft (80m) ▲▲▲
·LEVEL OF DIFFICULTY·	🚶 🚶 🚶
·PATHS·	Farm tracks, heathland paths, quiet roads, shingle beach
·LANDSCAPE·	Heathland, woodland, farmland, marshes and coast
·SUGGESTED MAP·	aqua3 OS Explorers 212 Woodbridge & Saxmundham; 231 Southwold & Bungay
·START / FINISH·	Grid reference: TM 478706 (on Explorer 231)
·DOG FRIENDLINESS·	On lead on National Trust land and Dingle Marshes
·PARKING·	Dunwich Beach free car park
·PUBLIC TOILETS·	At car park

BACKGROUND TO THE WALK

Medieval Dunwich was a splendid city and a major seaport that exported wool and grain to Europe and imported cloth and wine. It had six churches plus numerous chapels, convents, monasteries, hospitals, alehouses, farmhouses and mills. Now it is a small seaside village with a handful of houses and a pub. So where has it gone? The answer is that, like so much of the Suffolk coast, it has simply vanished into the sea.

The sea has been the making and breaking of Dunwich. It was the sea that provided the very reason for its existence and supported its industries of shipbuilding and fishing. It was the sea that brought its most famous figure, St Felix of Burgundy, a missionary invited by King Sigebert to preach Christianity to the pagans of East Anglia and rewarded with a bishopric and a cathedral at Dunwich in AD 630. It was the sea that silted up the harbour during a terrible storm in 1286, leading to the city's inevitable decline. And it is the sea, ever since, which has taken Dunwich back, a process which continues at the rate of around 1yd (1m) each year as the tides chip away at the base of the cliffs.

A scale model of the 12th-century city, housed in Dunwich Museum, reveals the full truth about its decline. The Roman town here extended 1 mile (1.6km) out to sea beyond the present coastline. Half of this had disappeared by the time of the Norman conquest but the worst was yet to come. The last church tumbled over the cliffs as recently as 1920 and the museum has a series of dramatic photographs showing it collapsing year by year. According to a local legend, you can still hear the bells of the sunken churches pealing beneath the sea on a stormy night.

Dunwich is a haunting place, where ghosts of the past assault your senses at every turn. High on the cliff near the start of the walk is the tombstone of Jacob Forster, all that remains of the churchyard of All Saints Church. The other graves have long since sunk without trace, and Jacob Forster's bones lie all alone. Who was he and what did he do to deserve such a fate? How long will it be until he goes too, to join his ancestors beneath the waves?

This walk also takes you to Dunwich Heath, where the National Trust manages a section of coastline as a conservation area. Come, if you can, between June and September, when the heathland on the cliff top is carpeted with glorious purple and pink heather.

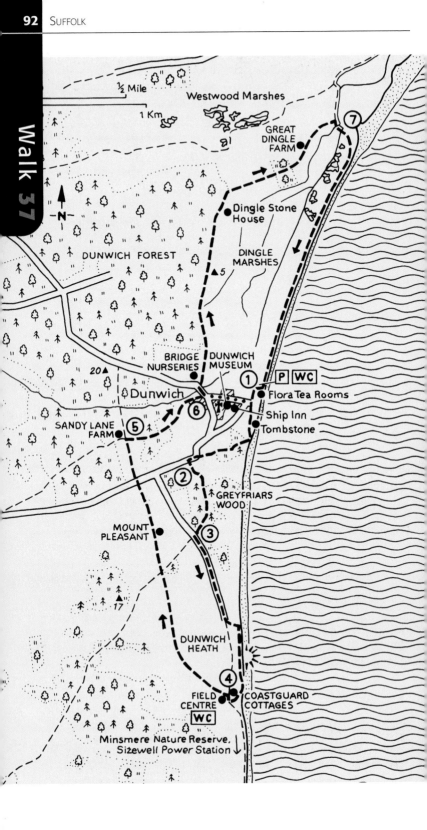

Walk 37

½ Mile
1 Km

Westwood Marshes

GREAT DINGLE FARM

Dingle Stone House

DUNWICH FOREST

DINGLE MARSHES

▲5

20▲

BRIDGE NURSERIES

DUNWICH MUSEUM

① P WC

Flora Tea Rooms

Dunwich

⑥

⑤

SANDY LANE FARM

Ship Inn
Tombstone

②

GREYFRIARS WOOD

③

MOUNT PLEASANT

▲17

④

DUNWICH HEATH

FIELD CENTRE

WC

COASTGUARD COTTAGES

Minsmere Nature Reserve,
Sizewell Power Station ↓

⑦

N

Walk 37 Directions

① Walk up the road from the beach car park and keep left at the junction. When the road bends, turn left on to a footpath that climbs through the woods to the ruins of **Greyfriars Friary**. Turn left along the cliff top, go over a set of wooden steps and bear right through the trees on a waymarked path. At the end of this path, turn right along a track to a road.

② Turn left off the road after 100yds (91m) on a track to the **Dairy House**. Keep straight ahead on this path as it enters **Greyfriars Wood** and continues to a road.

③ Turn left and walk along this road for ½ mile (800m), passing two caravan sites on the left. As soon as you enter National Trust land, turn left on to a path waymarked with white arrows.

④ Walk around the National Trust's **Coastguard Cottages** and take the track beside **Heath Barn field centre**, then bear right on to a sandy path that climbs through the heather. Keep on this path, bearing left and right at a crossing track to follow the Sandlings Walk nightjar waymarks. When you reach a bridleway, keep straight ahead on a

WHERE TO EAT AND DRINK ⓘ
The **Ship Inn** is an old smugglers' inn offering a varied menu. However, the really popular place to eat in summer is the **Flora Tea Rooms** on the beach. Expect to queue for fresh cod, haddock or lemon sole, served with chunky chips and eaten at tables on the terrace. The **National Trust** has a tea room in the Coastguard Cottages at Dunwich Heath.

farm track passing **Mount Pleasant** farm. Cross the road and keep straight ahead on a concrete lane to **Sandy Lane Farm**.

⑤ Turn right for ½ mile (800m) on a shady lane to emerge by **St James's Church**, built in the 19th century when other churches were falling into the sea. A short cut is to keep straight on to return to Dunwich.

⑥ Turn left at the road and, in 100yds (91m), go right at **Bridge Nurseries**. Keep to the right around the farm buildings and stay on this track for 1½ miles (2.4km) beside **Dunwich Forest** before turning seawards. Pass through a gate to enter a covert and fork right at a junction around **Great Dingle Farm**, then follow the path through the reed beds towards the sea.

⑦ Turn right at a junction, when you see an old drainage mill to your left, and follow the flood bank across **Dingle Marshes**. Turn right to return to **Dunwich** along the beach or take the path behind the shingle bank.

WHILE YOU'RE THERE ⓘ
Just south of Dunwich Heath is the **Minsmere Nature Reserve**, an area of marshes and lagoons that attracts numerous wading birds. Although there is a charge for entering the reserve, there is free access to the public hides from the coast path at Dunwich Heath.

Walk 38

Around the Lakes of the Cotswold Water Park

Through an evolving landscape in the southern Cotswolds.

•DISTANCE•	5 miles (8km)
•MINIMUM TIME•	2hrs
•ASCENT / GRADIENT•	Negligible
•LEVEL OF DIFFICULTY•	
•PATHS•	Track, tow path and lanes, 10 stiles
•LANDSCAPE•	Dead flat – lakes, light woodland, canal and village
•SUGGESTED MAP•	aqua3 OS Explorer 169 Cirencester & Swindon
•START / FINISH•	Grid reference: SU 048974
•DOG FRIENDLINESS•	Good but be aware of a lot of waterfowl around lakes
•PARKING•	Silver Street, South Cerney
•PUBLIC TOILETS•	None on route
•CONTRIBUTOR•	Christopher Knowles

BACKGROUND TO THE WALK

By their very nature, ancient landscapes and historic architecture evolve very slowly, changing little from one century to another. Can they resist the demands of a brasher era? In the Cotswolds the answer to this question is essentially 'yes'. Here building restrictions are strict – even, sometimes, draconian. The result, however, is a significant area of largely unspoilt English countryside; sometimes, thoughtful development has even enhanced an otherwise lacklustre skyline. The Cotswold Water Park, located in and around old gravel pits, is an example of this.

Recreational Gravel

Gravel has been worked in the upper Thames Valley, where the water table is close to the surface, since the 1920s. The removal of gravel leads to the creation of lakes and in the areas around South Cerney and between Fairford and Lechlade there are now some 4,000 acres (1,620ha) of water, in about 100 lakes. They provide an important wetland habitat for a variety of wildlife. Most of these lakes have been turned over to recreational use of one sort or another, being a perfect place for game and coarse fishing, board sailing, walking, boating of various kinds, riding and sundry other leisure activities. Interestingly, this has been what is now called a private/public enterprise. The landscaping has not just been a case of letting nature take over where the gravel excavators left off. The crane-grabs that were used for excavation in the 1960s, for example, left the gravel pits with vertical sides and therefore with deep water right up to the shoreline. As it happens, some forms of aquatic life flourish under these conditions, but in other lakes the shoreline has been graded to create a gentler slope, to harmonise better with the flat landscape in this part of the Cotswolds and to suit the needs of swimmers and children. In the same way, trees have been planted and hills have been constructed to offer shelter and visual relief. Old brick railway bridges have been preserved. Finally, a style of waterside architecture has been developed to attract people to live here. It continues to evolve, just as the surrounding countryside has done for centuries.

South Cerney and Cerney Wick

The walk begins in South Cerney, by the River Churn, only 4 miles (6.4km) from the source of the Thames. Look inside the Norman church for the exceptional carving on the 12th-century rood. Later the walk takes you through Cerney Wick, a smaller village on the other side of the gravel workings. The highlight here is an 18th-century roundhouse, used by the workers on the now disused Thames and Severn Canal.

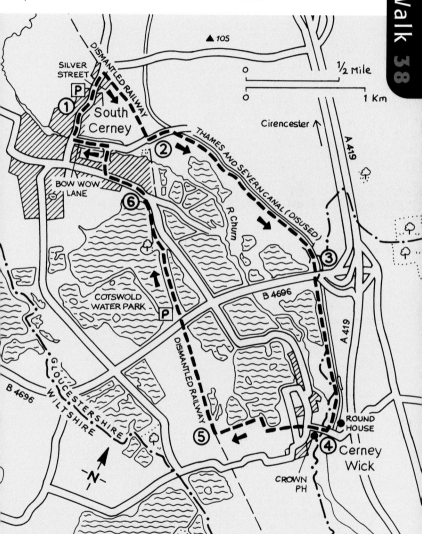

Walk 38 **Directions**

① From **Silver Street** walk north out of the village. Immediately before the turning to Driffield and Cricklade, turn right over a stile on to a bank. Stay on this obvious path for 800yds (732m), to reach a brick bridge across the path. Turn right here up a flight of steps to reach a narrow road.

WHERE TO EAT AND DRINK
The walk passes the **Crown** in Cerney Wick. There are also several pubs in South Cerney – the **Old George** and the **Eliot Arms** in Clarks Hay, and the **Royal Oak** on the High Street.

② Turn left and walk along here for 200yds (183m) until you come to footpaths to the right and left. Turn right along a farm track, following a signpost for **Cerney Wick**. Almost immediately the shallow, overgrown remains of the **Thames and Severn Canal** appear to your left. When the track veers right into a farm, walk ahead over a stile to follow a path beneath the trees – the old canal tow path. At a bridge keep ahead across stiles and continue until you come to a busy road.

③ Cross with care. On the far side you have two choices: either continue on the tow path or take the path that skirts the lakes. If you take the lakeside path, you will eventually be able to rejoin the tow path by going left at a bridge after 600yds (549m). Continue until, after just under ½ mile (800m), you pass an old canal roundhouse across the canal to the left and, soon after, reach a lane at **Cerney Wick**.

④ Turn right here and walk to the junction at the end of the road, beside the **Crown** pub. Cross to a stile and enter a field. Walk straight ahead and come to another stile. Cross this aiming to the left of a cottage. Cross the lane, go over another stile and enter a field. Walk ahead and follow the path as it guides you across a stile on to the grass by a lake. Walk around the lake, going right and then left. In the corner before you, cross into a field, walk ahead towards trees and cross a stile to a track.

⑤ Turn right, rejoining the **old railway line** and follow it to a road. Cross this into a car park and go through a gate on to a track. Stay on this to another road and follow a path that runs to its left.

⑥ Where the path ends at the beginning of **South Cerney**, continue along **Station Road**. Ignore a footpath on the right but turn right at the second one. Cross the bridge to a lane called '**Bow Wow**'. Turn left here between streams and return to **Silver Street**.

FOR BIRDWATCHERS
Reed bunting, sedge and reed warblers, and great crested grebes nest successfully around undisturbed vegetated margins within the park and sand martins excavate nest burrows in steep banks. During the winter months, duck numbers may exceed 20,000 so it is worth looking out for the occasional goosander or smew among flocks of tufted duck, pochard and gadwall.

WHAT TO LOOK FOR
Disused **transport systems** feature greatly in this walk. For much of it you will be beside or close to the old Thames and Severn Canal, or following the route of the old Andoversford railway line. The line linked Cheltenham and Swindon between 1891 and 1961. The **roundhouse** seen on the far side of the old canal as you approach Cerney Wick was used by lock keepers and maintenance engineers. This design was a distinctive feature of the Thames and Severn Canal. Even the windows were rounded to afford the occupants maximum visibility of their stretch of canal. The downstairs would have been used as a stable, the middle storey as a living area and the upstairs held sleeping accommodation.

Mines and Monasteries in Sandwell Valley Park

An easy walk around an RSPB nature reserve and a fine country park reveals a legacy of agriculture and industry.

Walk 39

•DISTANCE•	4 miles (6.4km)
•MINIMUM TIME•	1hr 30min
•ASCENT / GRADIENT•	66ft (20m) ▲ ▲ ▲
•LEVEL OF DIFFICULTY•	🚶🚶 🚶🚶 🚶🚶
•PATHS•	Lakeside paths and tracks, no stiles
•LANDSCAPE•	Country park with many lakes
•SUGGESTED MAP•	aqua3 OS Explorer 220 Birmingham
•START / FINISH•	Grid reference: SP 035927
•DOG FRIENDLINESS•	Off lead in park
•PARKING•	RSPB visitor centre
•PUBLIC TOILETS•	None on route

BACKGROUND TO THE WALK

Once upon a time there was a 12th-century Benedictine monastery on the site of an earlier hermitage in the area now called Sandwell Valley Country Park, situated at the north eastern edge of West Bromwich. The monastery was closed down in 1525 on the directions of Cardinal Wolsey, then in 1705 Sandwell Hall was erected on the site for the Earl of Dartmouth, incorporating some of the old priory buildings. The hall was demolished in 1928 with the development of Hamstead Colliery, which came to dominate the whole area. When the pit was nationalised in the 1940s it was one of the largest in South Staffordshire, outside Cannock Chase, with nearly 1,000 men working underground here and at the nearby Sandwell Park Colliery.

From Colliery to Country Park

The collieries closed in the early 1960s, since when the land has been transformed into an urban oasis. The earthworks became a series of artificial lakes and spoil from the site was landscaped to produce an amazingly different scene. Sandwell Valley Country Park is now a fascinating area of lakes and 2,000 acres (810ha) of parkland developed from the old colliery sites and the remains of the Sandwell Hall Estate. The park has become a major leisure facility, with three golf courses, walking routes, a Millennium Cycle Route and two off-road cycle paths which have been specially designed for mountain bikes. Around 20,000 people visit the park each year.

Attractive to Birds

Wildfowl flock to the area in large numbers and the Royal Society for the Protection of Birds (RSPB) has established a nature reserve here. The reserve covers some 25 acres (10ha) of the reclaimed Hamstead Colliery site and attracts around 150 species of bird each year. Throughout the year there are lapwings, grey herons, kingfishers, skylarks and goldfinches, while, in the summer months, spotted flycatchers, tree pipits and even orange-tip butterflies may put in an appearance. The RSPB work hard to promote public interest in the reserve, offering three free hides and maintaining a list of daily bird sightings. The River Tame meanders around Forge Mill Lake and attracts the large flocks of Canada geese out of the main reserve.

Victorian Farm

Forge Mill visitor centre can be found on the other side of Forge Lane, and Swan Pool leads to footbridges over the noisy M5 motorway. Sandwell Park Farm was also part of the Earl of Dartmouth's estate and was extensively restored in 1981 to show the traditional Victorian methods of farming. The farm has a walled kitchen garden, craft shops, a rare breeds area and a heritage centre where you can see the findings of a 1980s archaeological dig at Sandwell Priory. There are also toilets and tea rooms (➤ Where to Eat and Drink).

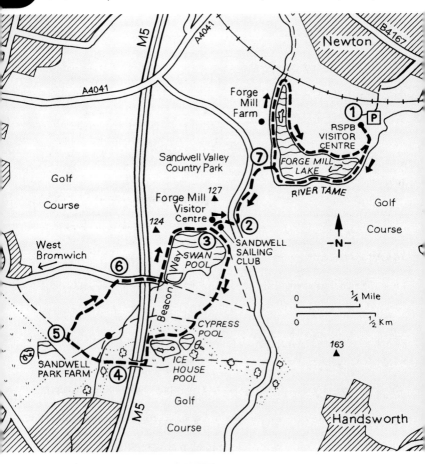

Walk 39 Directions

① Leave the **RSPB car park** by going left of the visitor centre building on to a footpath. This

leads down to a strip of land between the River Tame and **Forge Mill Lake**. Continue along the footpath which arcs gently right and look out for the many birds on the lake, as well as Canada geese

Walk 39

and ducks on the river. As you work your way around the lake you will come to a gateway where you go left over a bridge across the **River Tame** and continue on a tarmac path/cycleway that leads down to **Forge Lane**.

② Cross the busy lane with great care and walk to the right of the **Sandwell Sailing Club** premises, then bear left until you come to **Swan Pool**.

③ Head left and stroll around the side of the pool for 150yds (137m), then bear left again on to a footpath that leads across meadowland away from the water's edge. Soon you will enter a hedged footpath heading generally south west. At a junction of paths go left and proceed through the trees, then go right to follow the path to the north of **Cypress** and **Ice House pools**. You

will emerge on to a tarmac lane by the side of the noisy **M5**. (If you had continued ahead at the junction of paths instead of going left you would have arrived at the same position.) Go left and stroll along this wide lane. At a junction, bear right and take the footbridge over the M5.

④ Follow the tarmac path up to **Sandwell Park Farm** where there are toilet facilities and you can get light refreshments.

⑤ Go right, opposite to the farm buildings and walk along the signed public footpath heading north-eastwards into the trees. (To the left you will see a golf practice area.) When you reach the end of the hedged area bear left and proceed along a tarmac path until you reach a junction.

⑥ Go right here along **Salters Lane** and return over the **M5** via a second footbridge. Take the tarmac path that goes to the left of **Swan Pool** and continue past the sailing cub premises to busy **Forge Lane**. Cross the lane and take the footbridge back over the **River Tame** to reach the junction of footpaths by the edge of **Forge Mill Lake**.

⑦ Go left and walk around the lake back to the visitor centre.

Island Views from the Marloes Peninsula

An easy walk around a windswept headland overlooking two offshore islands and a marine nature reserve.

•DISTANCE•	6 miles (9.7km)
•MINIMUM TIME•	2hrs 30min
•ASCENT / GRADIENT•	420ft (128m) ▲ ⏶ ⏶
•LEVEL OF DIFFICULTY•	🚶🚶 🚶🚶 🚶
•PATHS•	Coast path and clear footpaths, short section on tarmac, 10 stiles
•LANDSCAPE•	Rugged cliff tops and beautiful sandy beaches
•SUGGESTED MAP•	aqua3 OS Explorer OL36 South Pembrokeshire
•START / FINISH•	Grid reference: SM 761089
•DOG FRIENDLINESS•	Poop scoop on beaches
•PARKING•	National Trust car park above Martin's Haven, near Marloes village
•PUBLIC TOILETS•	Marloes village

BACKGROUND TO THE WALK

The Marloes Peninsula forms the westernmost tip of the southern shores of St Brides Bay. The paddle-shaped headland is a popular place to walk due to the narrow neck that affords minimum inland walking for maximum time spent on the coast. It is famous for its stunning scenery, which includes two of the Pembrokeshire Coast National Park's finest and least-crowded beaches, some secluded coves that are often inhabited by seals, and wonderfully rugged coastline. There are also fine views over a narrow but turbulent sound to the small islands of Skomer and Skokholm – two significant seabird breeding grounds. The walking is captivating, even by Pembrokeshire standards.

Wildlife Sanctuary

Skomer is the largest of the Pembrokeshire islands and is one of the most significant wildlife habitats in the whole country. The island, separated from the mainland by the rushing waters of Jack Sound, measures approximately 1½ miles (2.4km) from north to south and 2 miles (3.2km) from east to west. It was declared a National Nature Reserve in 1959 and, as well as the protection it receives as part of the National Park, it's also designated as a Site of Special Scientific Interest (SSSI), a Special Protection Area (SPA) and a Geological Conservation Review Site (GCR). Much of the land is a Scheduled Ancient Monument, courtesy of a number of clearly visible Iron-Age settlements and enclosures. If that's not enough of an accolade, the sea that surrounds the island is a Marine Nature Reserve, one of only two in the United Kingdom; the other is Lundy, off the North Devon coast.

Puffins and Shearwaters

The two stars of the Skomer show are the diminutive but colourful puffin and the dowdy and secretive Manx shearwater. Puffins need little introduction; their colourful beaks and clown-like facial markings put them high on everybody's list of favourite birds. There are around 6,000 nesting pairs on Skomer. They arrive in April and lay a single egg in a burrow. The chick hatches at the end of May and the adult birds spend the next two months ferrying back catches of sand eels for their flightless offspring. After around seven weeks of this lavish attention the chick leaves the nest, usually at night, and makes its way to the sea. Assuming that it learns to look after itself successfully, it will spend the next few years at sea, only returning when it reaches breeding maturity.

Bashful Birds

The mouse-like shearwater is slightly larger than the puffin but it also lays its single egg in a burrow, overlooking the sea. It may not be as obviously endearing as its painted neighbour, especially as most visitors to the island never actually see one, but it's a beautiful and fascinating bird in its own right and there are in fact around 150,000 pairs on Skomer, Skokholm and Middleholm; which amounts to about 60 per cent of the world's total population. The reason they are seldom seen is because they are fairly vulnerable to predators on land so they leave the nest at dawn and spend the whole day at sea, not returning to their burrow until it's almost dark. A careful seawatch at last light may reveal them gathering in huge rafts just offshore or even endless lines of flying birds returning to the island – against the sunset, it's quite a magical sight.

Walk 40

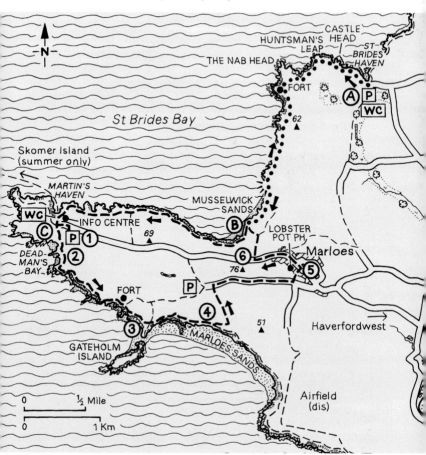

Walk 40 Directions

Walk 40

① From the car park turn left on to the road and walk down to the bottom of the hill. Bear around to the left, then go through the gate straight ahead into the **Deer Park**. Turn left and follow the path along to a stile and out on to the coast.

② With the sea to your right, continue easily along over **Deadman's Bay** to another stile. The next section cruises along easily, passing the earthworks of an Iron-Age fort on the left and crossing another stile as you approach **Gateholm Island**.

③ It is possible to get across to the island at low tide, but care is needed to scramble over the slippery rocks. To continue the walk, follow the coast path, above the western end of the beautiful **Marloes Sands** until you drop easily to the main beach access path.

WHERE TO EAT AND DRINK ℹ

The **Lobster Pot** in Marloes is conveniently placed at the halfway point of the walk, but no dogs or muddy boots, please. Alternatively, head for **Dale** or **Little Haven** at the end of the walk as both offer better options.

FOR BIRDWATCHERS

Marloes Peninsula is a migration hotspot for terrestrial songbirds but also one of the best places in Wales to observe movements of seabirds. From April to October auks, gannets, kittiwakes and Manx shearwaters move to and from nearby feeding and nesting grounds and in September unusual birds such as skuas and storm-petrels pass by on migration.

④ Turn left and climb up to the road; turn right here. Follow the road along for around ¾ mile (1.2km) to a bridleway on the left. Follow this down and turn left into **Marloes** village.

⑤ Pass the **Lobster Pot** on the left and continue ahead to leave the village. Ignore a few tracks on the right, as the road bends around to the left, and continue out into open countryside where you'll meet a footpath on the right.

⑥ Walk down the edge of the field and bear around to the left to drop back down on to the coast path above **Musselwick Sands**. Turn left and follow the path west for over 1½ miles (2.4km) to **Martin's Haven**. Meet the road and climb past the information centre back to the car park.

WHAT TO LOOK FOR ℹ

If you're walking along the coast in spring or summer you'll not fail to be impressed by the small white and pink flowers that carpet the cliff tops. These are **sea campion** (white) and **thrift** (pink), both common along the Pembrokeshire coast.

As you approach Musselwick Sands on Walk 41, you should be able to see a small island some 8 miles (12.9km) offshore. This is Grassholm and during the summer months it appears almost pure white. It isn't due to the colour of the rock but 30,000 breeding pairs of **gannets** that return to the island every year. Unlike the puffins and shearwaters of Skomer, the gannets are easily spotted, usually in small flocks, cruising a few hundred yards out looking for fish. If you spot them, watch closely and you'll probably witness their spectacular dive as they fold in their wings and plummet like darts into the water.

St Brides Haven and the Marloes Peninsula

An easy extension of Walk 40, starting at St Brides Haven and following more of the glorious coast path.
See map and information panel for Walk 40

•DISTANCE•	10 miles (16.1km)
•MINIMUM TIME•	4hrs 30min
•ASCENT / GRADIENT•	820ft (250m) ▲▲▲
•LEVEL OF DIFFICULTY•	🚶 🚶 🚶
•START / FINISH•	Grid Reference: SM 802108
•PARKING•	In front of church in St Brides Haven

Walk 41 Directions
(See Walk 40 map)

This walk extends the easy saunter around the peninsula described in Walk 40 by starting at St Brides Haven and following the coast path to Musselwick Sands, where the two walks merge. St Brides has a sheltered bay, ideal for an afternoon on the beach, and the coast path walking from here to Musselwick is both pretty and unusually flat. Although you can make this extension into a circuit by following footpaths north from Marloes village, the coast path is far more interesting.

From the church (Point **Ⓐ**) walk to the head of the inlet and turn left to cross the top of the beach and join the coast path as it climbs up to **Castle Head**. The path climbs upwards to **Huntsman's Leap**, a narrow cleft in the headland, and then goes south west towards **The Nab Head** where it finally heads south. Shortly after, you'll pass the remains of an Iron-Age fort.

The next section is straightforward with no navigation. Continue down into a dip and back up some steps to enjoy the views south to Skomer and Grassholm. Eventually, you'll pass above the beach that makes up **Musselwick Sands**. Drop into a steep sided dip and you'll meet a footpath coming in from the left. Here you join Walk 40 at Point **Ⓑ**.

Stay on the Coast Path to follow the instruction for Point **⑥** west to Point **Ⓒ**, at **Martin's Haven**. At the top of lane, stay on the coast path and pass through the gate in the wall, to follow Points **①** to **⑤**. These lead you to **Marloes Sands**, through **Marloes** and, on the first part of Point **⑥**, back to Point **Ⓑ**, where you turn right to retrace your steps to **St Brides Haven**.

FOR BIRDWATCHERS

In terms of marine life there are rich pickings for birds where the waves break on the beaches. It is worth scrutinising the flocks of black-headed and herring gulls that feed here for one of their more unusual cousins and look out for gleaming white sanderlings feeding right at the water's edge during winter.

Walk 42

The Pen y Fan Pilgrimage – a Circular Route

A straightforward circuit that follows the main trade routes up on to the roof of the National Park.

•DISTANCE•	5 miles (8km)
•MINIMUM TIME•	2hrs 30min
•ASCENT / GRADIENT•	1,610ft (491m) ▲▲▲
•LEVEL OF DIFFICULTY•	🚶🚶 🚶🚶 🚶🚶
•PATHS•	Clearly defined tracks, 2 stiles
•LANDSCAPE•	Rugged high mountains and deeply scooped valleys
•SUGGESTED MAP•	aqua3 OS Explorer OL12 Brecon Beacons National Park Western & Central areas
•START / FINISH•	Grid reference: SN 982203
•DOG FRIENDLINESS•	Care needed near sheep and on cliff tops
•PARKING•	Lay-by on A470, opposite Storey Arms and telephone box
•PUBLIC TOILETS•	¼ mile (400m) south of start

Walk 42 Directions

Every mountain has its 'trade route' – the easiest and most trafficked way to the top – and Pen y Fan is no different. This is the highest peak in southern Britain and the closest real mountain to a huge chunk of the population, attracting mass pilgrimages from the Home Counties, Birmingham and Bristol. The simple circular route described here, starts by crossing the head of the Taff Valley.

Cross the road and the stile next to the **telephone box**. The large building to your right is the **Storey Arms**, now an outdoor education centre but once a wayside inn on the coaching road between Brecon and South Wales. The original road can be seen forking off to your left, this forms a section of the Taff Trail, a long distance route between Cardiff and Brecon. Follow a clear,

in places artificial, path up the hillside, leaving the plantation behind and crossing the open moorland of the southern flanks of **Y Gyrn** – a rounded summit to your left. You'll soon gain the ridge and cross a stile to drop easily down to the infant **Taf Fawr** – a pleasant spot, ideal for a break before you reach the exposed hilltops above. The way ahead is clear, with the rough and eroded track climbing steeply up the hillside opposite. Follow this until it reaches the escarpment edge above the magnificent valley of **Cwm Llwch**. Below you'll see the glacier-formed lake of Llyn Cwm Llwch, and above this the steep head wall that unites the twin peaks.

Turn right to follow the clear path up towards the rocky ramparts of **Corn Du**. The path slips easily around the craggy outcrops and leads you up to the huge cairn on top of the broad summit plateau. The views down the valley are

Walk 42

leads to the summit. The views from this section are to the south, over the two Neuadd reservoirs. Bwlch Duwynt represents a fairly major junction of paths, but you'll easily locate the main track that leads downhill to your right, away from Corn Du. Again, sections of this track have been laid in stone in recent years to restrict the erosion caused by thousands of walkers' feet. Follow the track down for just

awesome, but take care as some of the summit rocks overhang.

The way to **Pen y Fan** is obvious from here. Drop into the shallow saddle to the east and continue easily on to the summit. This opens up a whole new vista, with the narrow ridge of **Cefn Cwm Llwch** acting as the dividing wall for the remote **Cwm Sere**, to the right as you look out.

The north east face of the mountain is particularly precipitous so take care near the edges. The most enjoyable way to begin your descent is to retrace your steps across Corn Du to **Bwlch Duwynt**, the obvious saddle between the summit and the long ridge that runs south. An alternative is the good path which runs below Corn Du, allowing easy passage with no extra height gain. To locate this, drop back into the saddle you've just crossed and fork left, beneath the grassy slope that

over a mile (1.6km) until you see the **Taf Fawr** river on your right.

A short diversion to your right just here will reveal a great picnic spot, situated above a waterfall. Continue down to ford the river and go through the kissing gate into the main car park. Turn right into the car park and follow it to its end where a gravel footpath (signposted with a **Taff Trail** waymarker) takes over. Continue along the side of the plantation and cross the road to return to the start.

Around Carsington Reservoir

Derbyshire's most controversial modern reservoir is now a magnet for wildlife.

•DISTANCE•	8 miles (12.9km)
•MINIMUM TIME•	4hrs
•ASCENT / GRADIENT•	Negligible
•LEVEL OF DIFFICULTY•	
•PATHS•	Surfaced and unsurfaced waymarked paths, a few stiles
•LANDSCAPE•	Reservoir and low pastured hillsides
•SUGGESTED MAP•	aqua3 OS Outdoor Leisure 24 White Peak
•START / FINISH•	Grid reference: SK 241516
•DOG FRIENDLINESS•	Severn Trent Water ask that dogs be kept on leads
•PARKING•	Carsington Reservoir visitor centre car park
•PUBLIC TOILETS•	At car park

Walk 43 Directions

Planned in the 1960s and argued about well into the 1970s, **Carsington Reservoir** was finally inaugurated by the Queen in 1992. Built in a shallow valley with a poor catchment area, the reservoir's main supply is pumped from the River Derwent at Ambergate and conveyed 6½ miles (10.4km) down a pipeline. When the Derwent's water levels are low, water is pumped in the opposite direction.

Severn Trent Water has built a state-of-the-art visitor centre, a sports and activity centre, a restaurant, some shops and a sailing club. They boast about good conservation policies and pure clean water. But somehow you get that sinking feeling as you cross the vast car park in search of a walk.

The gloom's short-lived however, for once you're past **Millbank** at the southern end of the lake, you will leave the tarmac behind and you start to see the wildlife – a swan, a moorhen, a grebe. And soon after that you're walking among wetlands and through woods, looking across a very pleasant blue to verdant hillslopes.

From the visitor centre follow the signposted bridleway southwards past the sailing club and across the huge dam, which holds back 7.8 billion gallons (35.5 billion litres) of

FOR BIRDWATCHERS

In spring and autumn, a surprising range of migrant birds turn up at Carsington, attracted by the water and the prospect of being able to feed. Autumn can be particularly rewarding for waders if water levels are low and muddy margins are exposed: little stint and curlew sandpiper have been recorded along with other species more usually associated with the seashore, such as turnstone and knot.

water. When full the reservoir is 100ft (30m) deep covering an area the size of 700 football pitches.

At the far end of the dam the tarmac path reaches **Millfields**, where there is a refreshment kiosk (seasonal). From here a path with yellow markers continues close to the reservoir shoreline, passing the car park and reacquainting itself with the bridleway on several occasions. After crossing a footbridge over wetlands the path comes to a narrow tarmac lane by **Upperfields Farm**.

Turn left along the lane, then right at a gate, following a track, signposted to **Hopton**. The winding track dips and climbs high above the sinuous lakeshore, passing through pastureland and into the shade of woodland.

The track turns left at the northern end of the lake, then left again parallel to the main road. Cross the road, before continuing along the track on the other side. This leads northwards into **Hopton** village, where you turn left into neighbouring **Carsington**.

The **Miners Arms** doesn't look much from the road, but you walk through the car park and find that the front is at the back and it's a good looking pub with a pleasant beer garden.

FOR BIRDWATCHERS

The American ruddy duck, which has a reddish back, white cheeks and large blue bill, is a regular on Carsington Water. The little duck escaped from the Wildlife Trust and is now threatening to overrun native species, such as the European white-headed duck.

The walk continues south on a track just beyond the pub's car park. Turn left along the lane behind the pub, then right past **Wash Farm** and back to the main road. Across the road, follow the left fork path, which leads to **Sheepwash** car park.

Take the waymarked path between the metalled car park loop roads and continue south west, by-passing the conservation area.

There are a couple of signposted detours to waterside hides. The reservoir is quickly establishing itself as a haven for wildfowl. Wigeon, pochard and tufted ducks regularly winter here, while in the summer you will probably see great crested grebes. There are also cormorants and elegant grey herons. The watchtower, which provides a good place for viewing the bird life, was built as an observation post during the Second World War.

Beyond the second hide the path meets and then joins the bridleway, but gives it the slip again to cut a corner round one of the inlets. The ways continue to flirt with each other like this until you reach the wildlife centre, where you should opt for the the bridleway to take you back to the visitor centre.

WHERE TO EAT AND DRINK (i)

The **Miners Arms** is a pleasant 400 year-old pub with a large beer garden. It serves good sandwiches and bar meals. You can gaze across Carsington Water while you eat at the visitor centre's **Barrowdale Restaurant**. It is licensed and serves morning coffee, pleasant lunches and afternoon teas.

Gisburn Forest – a Walk in the Woods

Wooded valleys and heathland – accompanied by the sounds of woodland birds and waterfowl.

•DISTANCE•	3 miles (4.8km)
•MINIMUM TIME•	1hr 30min
•ASCENT / GRADIENT•	285ft (87m)
•LEVEL OF DIFFICULTY•	
•PATHS•	Forest tracks and footpaths
•LANDSCAPE•	Wooded valleys, forest, beckside heathland
•SUGGESTED MAP•	aqua3 OS Explorer OL41 Forest of Bowland & Ribblesdale
•START / FINISH•	Grid reference: SD 732565
•DOG FRIENDLINESS•	Fine for dogs under reasonable control
•PARKING•	Stocks Reservoir car park, Gisburn Forest (free of charge)
•PUBLIC TOILETS•	None on route
•CONTRIBUTOR•	Sheila Bowker

BACKGROUND TO THE WALK

Perfectly placed between the Yorkshire Dales and the Forest of Bowland, Gisburn Forest in the Upper Hodder Valley is the setting for this short, circular stroll. Don't be put off because it's in a forest – it certainly isn't a dire trek through the darkness of a dense conifer plantation. You will walk along open, naturally wooded valleys, beside a tumbling beck and over heathland. You will have views over the reservoir and up to the fells, and you will hear the woodland birdsong and the call of the wildfowl on the water. If you're lucky, you may spot a deer, footprints in the sandy earth confirm their presence.

Stocks Reservoir

The two defining aspects of this walk are the open waters of Stocks Reservoir and the woodlands of Gisburn Forest. The reservoir was built in the 1930s to provide drinking water for the towns of central Lancashire. The village of Stocks was submerged in the process along with many ancient farmsteads. The date stone from one of these can now be seen over the doorway of the post office in Tosside. It was formed by damming the River Hodder and can hold 2.6 billion gallons (12 billion litres) of water when it is at full capacity.

Attractively placed on the edge of the forest, the reservoir is now an important site for wildfowl and other wetland birds and 30 different species visit during the average winter period. Amongst the less-commonly sighted of these are red-throated divers, whooper swans, gadwalls and great crested grebes. Peregrine falcons have been spotted here as well as a rare passing marsh harrier and osprey. A birdwatching hide is provided for ornithologists, and a pleasant permissive footpath has been constructed around the shoreline.

The Forestry Commission's extensive woodland known as Gisburn Forest was developed at the same time as the reservoir and was opened by HRH Prince George in July 1932. It covers 3,000 acres (1,214ha), making it the largest single forested area in Lancashire. There are several waymarked trails to be enjoyed, and a cycle network has been developed extending to over 10 miles (16km). Although the majority of the plantations are of the monotonous coniferous variety and are managed principally as a commercial crop, more and more broadleaf trees are being planted to improve the visual aspect and to increase the diversity of wildlife. The forest and the reservoir are now managed in tandem, with inputs from United Utilities, the Forestry Commission and local parishes, to develop a sustainable economic base for this beautiful landscape.

Walk 44

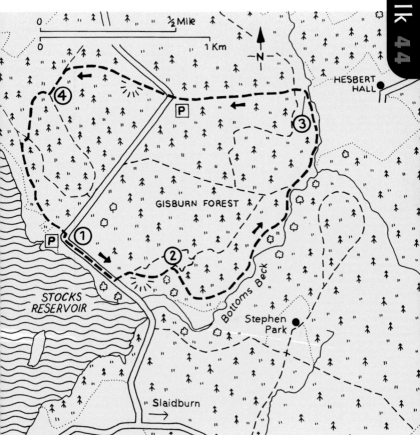

Walk 44 **Directions**

① Leave **Stocks Reservoir car park** in a south easterly direction (straight ahead from the right of the two vehicular entrances). Walk for approximately ¼ mile (400m) then turn left on a forest track marked with a wooden public footpath sign; a red marker post soon confirms your route. There are

good views right, through the trees to the reservoir and causeway with the fells in the background. Keep on the track as it takes you beside open wooded valleys and through natural woodland with a river down on your right.

② Follow the red marker post, set a little off to the right, as it leads you down on to a footpath. The footpath continues with a stream

Walk 44

on your left, across a low footbridge to the opposite bank. Soon the tumbling peaty **Bottoms Beck** is on your right with patches of reeds to the left, until a raised embankment leads to higher ground as you pass the farmland of **Hesbert Hall** to the right.

③ Follow the next red marker post as it directs you left to leave the beck, and walk just a few paces to cross straight over a forest track. Follow the path as it takes you gently uphill over boardwalks and heathland, through upright gateposts by an old broken down wall. Walk straight through **Swinshaw Top** car park to the road and go straight over to take a narrow footpath through the woods by another red marker post. The path opens on to a broadish green swathe but is soon closed in again; however lovely elevated views over the reservoir, left, and the fells ahead make the start of your descent pleasurable.

④ Meet a forest track at a bend, proceed straight ahead (slightly right) and follow the track for 200yds (183m) until red posts turn you right, down a footpath with a stream on the right. At a T-junction of footpaths, turn left across open heathland on a clear path back to the car park.

Meres, Mosses and Moraines at Ellesmere

A wonderful watery walk through Shropshire's lake district.

•DISTANCE•	7¼ miles (11.7km)
•MINIMUM TIME•	3hrs
•ASCENT / GRADIENT•	180ft (55m) ▲ ▲ ▲
•LEVEL OF DIFFICULTY•	🚶🚶 🚶 🚶
•PATHS•	Field paths and canal tow path, 8 stiles
•LANDSCAPE•	Pastoral hills with glacial hollows containing small lakes
•SUGGESTED MAP•	aqua3 OS Explorer 241 Shrewsbury
•START / FINISH•	Grid reference: SJ 407344
•DOG FRIENDLINESS•	Can run free on tow path, but under tight control elsewhere
•PARKING•	Castlefields car park opposite The Mere
•PUBLIC TOILETS•	Next to The Mere, almost opposite car park

BACKGROUND TO THE WALK

Ellesmere is another of those delightful little towns in which Shropshire specialises. It's well worth devoting some time to exploring it. But Ellesmere's biggest asset must be The Mere, the largest of all the meres that grace north Shropshire and south Cheshire. It attracts good numbers of water birds and is especially important for winter migrants such as wigeon, pochard, goosander and teal. It also has a large heronry occupied by breeding birds in spring and early summer.

On this walk you will explore about half of The Mere's shoreline and follow the tow path of the Llangollen Canal past Cole Mere and Blake Mere. Cole Mere is included within a country park and there is access from the tow path at Yell Bridge (54). If you want to explore Cole Mere, you can walk all the way round it. Blake Mere is particularly lovely; it's separated from the tow path only by a narrow strip of woodland, but there is no other access to it.

Glacial Formations

The word mere is an Anglo-Saxon term for a lake. Unlike a normal lake, however, these meres have no stream flowing in or out of them. So how were they formed? It's a complex story but the Meres Visitor Centre has lots of information. What follows here is a simplified version. During the last ice age, the landscape was scoured by glaciers and when they retreated between 10,000 to 12,000 years ago, they left clay-lined hollows which retained melting ice, forming some of the meres. Others filled up later because they lay below the level of the water table. Water levels are maintained by natural drainage (groundwater percolation) from the surrounding countryside.

The landscape is composed of gentle hills that, combined with the meres, form a very pleasing scene. Technically, it consists of glacial drift, a mixture of clays, sands and gravels originally scoured from rocks by the glaciers as they moved south and east across Britain and then deposited in banks and mounds known as moraines as the glaciers retreated. In places, you can identify the origins of the glacial drift. Blue-black pebbles are slates from Snowdonia or Cumbria, and pale, speckled stones are granites from Cumbria or Scotland, while pink pebbles are from the local sandstone. These glacial meres are unique in this country and rare in global terms.

North Shropshire is also renowned for its mosses, which were created by the glaciers too, but they are filled with peat rather than water. If you've done Walk 2 you'll be familiar with the wonderful moss at Whixall, but there are several small mosses around Ellesmere too, though none with public access. The meres and mosses together form a wetland complex which, ecologically, is of national, if not international, significance.

① Cross to **The Mere** and turn left. Pass **The Boathouse** and **Meres**

Visitor Centre and walk towards town, until you come to **Cremorne Gardens**. Join a path that runs through trees close by the water's edge for about ¾ mile (1.2km).

② Leave the trees for a field and turn left, signposted 'Welshampton'. The path soon joins a track, which leads to **Crimps Farm**. Turn right past the farm buildings to cross a stile on the right of the track. Continue along another track.

③ The track leads into sheep pasture where you go straight on, guided by waymarkers and stiles. When you come to a field with a **trig pillar** in it, the waymarker is slightly misleading – ignore it and go straight across. In the next field you should aim for three prominent trees close together at the far side. As you approach them, turn left into the field corner.

WHERE TO EAT AND DRINK ⓘ

There is plenty of choice in Ellesmere. Special mention goes to **Vermeulen's** bakery/deli where you can buy the ingredients for a picnic. Or there's **The Boathouse** by The Mere, an unusual oak-beamed 1930s restaurant/tea room. There's a good range of snacks and drinks on offer, and dogs are welcome in the garden, which borders The Mere.

---

④ Go through a gate and descend by the right-hand hedge. When it turns a corner, go with it, to the right. Skirt a pool and keep going in the same direction on a grassy track, passing another pool. The track soon becomes much better defined and leads to a farm where you join a road.

⑤ Turn left and go straight on at a junction into **Welshampton**. Turn right on **Lyneal Lane** and follow it to a bridge over the **Llangollen Canal**. Descend steps to the tow path and turn right, passing under the bridge. Pass Lyneal Wharf, Cole Mere, Yell Wood and Blake Mere, then through **Ellesmere Tunnel**.

FOR BIRDWATCHERS

Given the terrain and landscape it is hardly surprising that ornithological interest is concentrated near water on this walk. In addition to species that are tied to water – grebes and ducks for example – look out for swallows, sand martins and swifts that visit the area to feed on insects. In winter, scrutinise duck flocks for the occasional scaup or goldeneye.

Beyond this are three footpaths signposted to The Mere. Take any of these short cuts if you wish, but to see a bit more of the canal, including the visitor moorings and marina, stay on the tow path.

⑥ Arriving at **bridge 58**, further choices present themselves. You could extend this walk to include the signposted Wharf Circular Walk (recommended) or to explore the town (also recommended): just follow the signs. To return directly to The Mere, however, go up to the road and turn left.

⑦ Fork right on a road by **Blackwater Cottage**. Turn right at the top, then soon left at **Rose Bank**, up steps. Walk across the earthworks of the long-gone **Ellesmere Castle** and follow signs for The Mere or the car park.

FOR BIRDWATCHERS

Many bird species can be seen, but one of the most endearing is the **great crested grebe**. This distinctive diving bird is nearly always present on the larger meres. You can recognise it by the crest on top of its head. In spring it has cute, stripy chicks which it sometimes carries on its back to give them a rest from all that paddling.

Walk 46

High Arnside Knott

This tree-clad knoll offers astonishing views and a special ambience.

•DISTANCE•	5½ miles (8.8km)
•MINIMUM TIME•	3hrs
•ASCENT / GRADIENT•	560t (170m) ▲▲ ▲
•LEVEL OF DIFFICULTY•	🏃 🏃 🏃
•PATHS•	Foreshore, paths, some surfaced road, 2 stiles
•LANDSCAPE•	Estuary and foreshore, mixed woods, limestone knoll
•SUGGESTED MAP•	aqua3 OS Explorer OL 7 The English Lakes (SE)
•START / FINISH•	Grid reference: SD 454786
•DOG FRIENDLINESS•	Generally a good walk for energetic dogs
•PARKING•	Free parking along promenade
•PUBLIC TOILETS•	Above road located centrally along Arnside's sea front
•NOTE •	Parts of foreshore impassable at high tide, beware of rapidly incoming tides and quicksand; some unguarded little crags
•CONTRIBUTOR•	Bill Birkett

Walk 46 Directions

Rising from the Kent Estuary to form a defiant outpost of resilient limestone, the heights of Arnside Knott are deservedly classed as an Area of Outstanding Natural Beauty. Bedecked with magnificent oak and mixed woods, rocky scree, hummocky grass, scattered bushes and the airy delights of steep open hillside, they also have the salty tang of the Kent Estuary which floods out into Morecambe Bay. Above the trees, to the north, the panoramic view of the high fells of Lakeland is nothing short of spectacular.

The little town of Arnside, with its station, viaduct crossing the estuary and elegant white limestone buildings, exudes a quiet feeling of Victorian affluence. As a child I was always thrilled by the tales of 'treading for fluke', literally fishing for the flatfish of that name, using your feet to hold them in place

before scooping them out with your hands, and the terrors of the Arnside Bore. The former has been replaced by lines of conventional anglers equipped with modern tackle. The latter, a wave which runs in at the front of a rising tide, still presents a dramatic sight plus great danger out on the sands here, as the tide floods in at a gallop. A warning siren is sounded at the start of an incoming tide – heed its call.

Walk along the **promenade** until, at the end of the surfaced road, by the entrance to **Ash Meadow House**, a walkway to the right continues above the sands. Continue along the path until it joins the foreshore. Continuing beneath **Grubbins**

> **WHERE TO EAT AND DRINK** ⓘ
>
> **Ye Olde Fighting Cocks**, a traditional inn whose name tells its own tale about the history of the region, is situated centrally on the sea front and offers bar meals and real ales. Also on the front, near the end of the walk, is the **Bay View Bakery and Café**.

> **WHAT TO LOOK FOR** ⓘ
>
> The oak woods, open tussocky grassland and scrub of this high limestone knoll are noted for their **butterflies**, and some 27 species are regularly seen here. Of particular interest are Scotch argus, on the wing between July and early August and the high brown fritillary in late June or early July. The latter, which has suffered decline elsewhere, still holds strong here.

Wood, the path crosses mud, pebbles and a polished limestone outcrop, before it rounds a little headland to join a track. Bear right to **New Barns**. Leave the track and pass the buildings on the right following the foreshore, signed 'Public footpath subject to tides'. Round **Frith Wood**, following the path beneath the trees, high on the pebble beach. Keep on to rocky **Blackstone Point**. If the tide is high it's possible to climb to the path above the little cliffs and continue along the edge of the wood. Round the point and enter the little bay to walk along its brilliant white pebbles. It is usual to ascend here to follow the path above the little edge along the fringe of the woods of **Arnside Park**. Depending on the tide, it may seem attractive to walk along the sands beneath the cliffs. This isn't recommended as quicksands are prevalent here and are undetectable until you sink.

Round **Park Point** and continue along the edge. At a junction with a ruined stone wall, a track leads steeply up to the left to join another track in the woods, signed 'Far Arnside, Silverdale'. Go right and continue, to join a road and a caravan site. Keep left along a high road and continue, to exit the site. Go along the road until a squeeze stile and gate lead through the wall

on the left, signed 'Public footpath Arnside via The Knott'. Walk through the fields to **Hollins Farm**, go through a stile gate on to a lane.

Go left up the lane and exit by a gate. Bear right following the path up the hillside of **Heathwaite**. A gate leads through the wall and out on to a track in the woods. Go straight across and ascend the stony track, continuing up into **Arnside Knott Wood**. Where the path levels at a junction of tracks, go left to emerge from the trees and make a slight descent to a toposcope. Return to the junction and continue along the shoulder to ascend to a bench near the summit. A path rising to the right leads to the trig point.

Go left, descend the path to a gate leading through the wall and continue straight down the field of **Red Hills**. Bear right to the bottom right corner of the field where a gate enters the woods. Descend the track through the woods to emerge on a road. Keep left until a road bears sharp right to descend to a larger road. Go right along this for a short way to join the Silverdale road. Bear left down to the seafront.

> **FOR BIRDWATCHERS** 🐦
>
> The expanse of Morecambe Bay is rich in marine life and provides food for countless tens of thousands of birds. As the rising tide pushes them closer to land, look for redshank, oystercatcher, dunlin, sanderling, curlew and turnstone; numbers are highest between October and March. During spring and summer, a highlight of the wooded slopes of Arnside Knott is the redstart, a migrant visitor to the region.

Bamburgh's Coast and Castle

Enjoy a fine beach, rolling countryside and superb views to Bamburgh Castle and the Farne Islands.

•DISTANCE•	8½ miles (13.7km)
•MINIMUM TIME•	3hrs 15min
•ASCENT / GRADIENT•	450ft (137m) ▲▲ ▲▲ ▲▲
•LEVEL OF DIFFICULTY•	🚶 🚶 🚶
•PATHS•	Field paths, dunes and beach, 10 stiles
•LANDSCAPE•	Coastal pasture and dunes
•SUGGESTED MAP•	aqua3 OS Explorer 340 Holy Island & Bamburgh
•START / FINISH•	Grid reference: NU 183348
•DOG FRIENDLINESS•	Can be off leads on dunes and beach
•PARKING•	Pay-and-display parking by Bamburgh Castle
•PUBLIC TOILETS•	Bamburgh
•CONTRIBUTOR•	Dennis Kelsall

BACKGROUND TO THE WALK

For as long as people have sailed this coast, the Farne Islands have been a hazard, claiming countless lives on their treacherous rocks. The most easterly outcrop of Northumberland's whinstone intrusion, they form two main groups and comprise around 30 tilted, low-lying islands, some barely breaking the waves. Their harsh environment and isolated position attracted the early Christian saints, who sought seclusion for a life of prayer and meditation. And on Inner Farne, the largest of the group, is a restored 14th-century chapel dedicated to St Cuthbert, who spent the last years of his life there.

The Early Lighthouses

The first attempt to mark the Farne Islands for shipping was around 1673, when a signal fire was lit on a 16th-century tower, built by the Bishop of Durham, on Inner Farne. Later, other beacon towers were built, first on Staple Island and then, in 1783, on Brownsman. The first modern lighthouse was erected on Inner Farne in 1809 and was quickly followed by another on Brownsman. However, the latter actually proved a danger and was replaced in 1826 with one on Longstone. Sadly, even these efficient lights were unable to prevent every disaster, and ships continued to founder on the dangerous reefs. The event that caught the imagination of the country, though, was the wreck of the SS *Forfarshire* in 1838 because of the unstilted heroism of the Longstone keeper and his daughter in rescuing the survivors. The Darlings had been keepers of the Farne lights since 1795, when Robert was appointed to the Brownsman beacon. He later took over the new lighthouse and was followed by his son William in 1815, who then moved to the new light on Longstone when it opened.

An Heroic Rescue

A storm was raging before dawn on 7 September 1838 when the *Forfarshire* struck Big Harcar, just south west of Longstone. William's daughter, Grace, was keeping watch with her father and spotted the wreck, although at first neither could see any survivors. With first light, they sighted men clinging to the wave-washed rock and launched their tiny coble to attempt a rescue. They found nine survivors, including a woman, but were only able to bring five back on the first trip. William returned with two of them for those remaining, whilst his daughter helped the others recover from their exposure. Grace became a national heroine, but managed to remain unaffected by the publicity and stayed with her parents at Bamburgh. Sadly, she died of tuberculosis only four years later at the age of 26. A small museum in the village tells the story and, in the churchyard opposite, there is a replica of the memorial effigy that was placed near her grave, the original having been removed inside the church for protection.

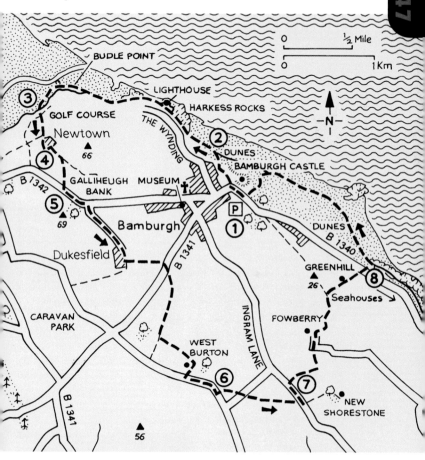

① Walk towards **Bamburgh** village, where you'll find the museum and church. Our route, however, continues along the beach, reached either across the green below the

castle or by following **The Wynding**, just beyond, and then crossing the dunes behind.

② To the left, the sand soon gives way to **Harkess Rocks**. Carefully pick your way round to the **lighthouse** at Blackrocks Point,

Walk 47

which is more easily negotiated to the landward side. Continue below the dunes, shortly regaining a sandy beach to pass around **Budle Point**.

③ Shortly before a derelict pier, climb on to the dunes towards a World War Two gun emplacement, behind which a waymarked path rises on to a golf course. Continue past markers to a gate, leaving along a track above a caravan park. At a bend, go through a gate on the left (marked 'Private') and carry on at the edge of the field to reach the cottages at **Newtown**.

④ Beyond, follow a wall on the left to regain the golf course over a stile at the top field-corner. Bear right to pass left of a look-out and continue on a grass track to the main road.

⑤ Walk down **Galliheugh Bank** to a bend and turn off to **Dukesfield**.

FOR BIRDWATCHERS 🐦
Coastal birds are the main attraction of this walk. Budle Bay (viewed from Budle Point) harbours vast mudflats and its lugworm population feeds hungry curlews and godwits during the winter months. Along the exposed shores towards Bamburgh Castle, look for groups of eider ducks, passing kittiwakes, and turnstones feeding along the tideline.

Approaching the lane's end, go left over a stile, walk past a house to the field's far corner and continue by a hedge to a road. Cross to follow a green lane opposite and eventually, just after a cottage, reach a stile on the left. Make for **West Burton farm**, turn right through the farmyard to a lane and then go left.

⑥ Beyond a bend and over a stile on the left, signed 'New Shorestone', bear half-right across a field. Emerging on to a quiet lane, go over another stile opposite and continue in the same direction to **Ingram Lane**.

WHERE TO EAT AND DRINK ⓘ
Places to choose from in the village include the **Lord Crewe Arms**, **Castle Hotel**, **Victoria House Brasserie** and the **Copper Kettle Tea Rooms**, between them they offer everything from morning coffee to a full evening dinner. If you visit the castle, you'll also find refreshments served in the tea room.

⑦ Some 300yds to the left (274m), a gated track on the right leads away and then around to the left towards **Fowberry**. Meeting a narrow lane, go left to the farm, then turn right immediately before the entrance on to a green track. In the next field, follow the left perimeter around the corner to a metal gate. Through that, remain beside the right-hand wall to a double gate, there turning right across a final field to **Greenhill**. Keep ahead to the main road.

⑧ Continue across to the beach and head north to Bamburgh. Approaching the castle, turn inland, over the dunes, where a cattle fence can be crossed by one of several gates or stiles. Work your way through to regain the road by the car park.

A Trail Through the Sallochy Woods

A gentle stroll by the bonnie banks of Loch Lomond.

•DISTANCE•	2 miles (3.2km)
•MINIMUM TIME•	2hrs 30min
•ASCENT / GRADIENT•	131ft (40m)
•LEVEL OF DIFFICULTY•	
•PATHS•	West Highland Way, forest trail and forest road
•LANDSCAPE•	Loch, hills and woodland
•SUGGESTED MAP•	aqua3 OS Explorer 364 Loch Lomond North
•START / FINISH•	Grid reference: NS 380957
•DOG FRIENDLINESS•	Suitable for dogs
•PARKING•	Sallochy Woods car park
•PUBLIC TOILETS•	None on route
•CONTRIBUTORS•	Hugh Taylor and Moira McCrossan

BACKGROUND TO THE WALK

One of Scotland's best-known songs, *The Bonnie Banks of Loch Lomond*, was reputedly written by a soldier of Prince Charles Edward Stuart's army during the Jacobite rising of 1745. During the long, slow retreat from Derby the soldier was captured and taken to Carlisle Castle and it was here that he wrote the song for his love, while languishing in prison awaiting execution. It tells of their joy in each other's company on the banks of Loch Lomond and how she would make the lonely journey home to Scotland by the 'high road'. Meanwhile his soul would be instantly transported at the moment of death back to his beloved loch along the 'low road' of the underworld and reach there before her. It's a poignant song of love and parting and a nostalgic remembrance of a landscape that the soldier will never see again in life.

Loch Lomond
Loch Lomond is the largest fresh water lake in Britain. It is 24 miles (38.6km) long, 5 miles (8km) wide and, at its deepest point is 623ft (190m) deep. Within its banks are approximately 38 islands, some of which are inhabited while others form sanctuaries for birds and wildlife. Most of them are in private ownership and not open to visitors. Inchcailloch is part of the National Nature Reserve and Bucinch and Ceardach are National Trust for Scotland properties. They can be visited and in summer a ferry and mail boat operate a regular passenger service from the boatyard at Balmaha, allowing island exploration and the opportunity to lunch at the Inchmurrin Hotel on Inchmurrin.

Geological Fault
The loch straddles the Highland Boundary Fault, a fracture caused by movement of the earth's crust millions of years ago, and the geological differences between Highland and Lowland Scotland are clearly visible from its banks. Here the fault runs from Conic Hill on the south east shore through the islands of Inchcailloch, Torrinch, Creinch and Inchmurrin.

Forest Park

Most visitors rush up the busy A82 along the west side of Loch Lomond, but on the more secluded eastern shore there is a largely unspoilt area of tranquillity and beauty, even in the height of summer. The diverse woods here are part of the Queen Elizabeth Forest Park and contain walking and nature trails and isolated picnic spots. The variety of animals and plants which can be found is staggering. Over a quarter of the plants that flourish in Britain can be found around the loch. You may well spot the rare capercaillie (it's the size of a turkey), ptarmigan or even a golden eagle. On Inchcailloch white fallow deer have been spotted in the past.

Walk 48 **Directions**

① From the car park head towards the entrance on to the main road. Go right on to a track beside the starting post to the **Sallochy Trail**. Cross the road with care and continue along the trail on the other side. This runs alongside some woodland which you should keep on your your right-hand side. Continue and, when the path eventually forks, keep right and go into the wood following the obvious waymarker posts.

WHILE YOU'RE THERE ⓘ
Head for **Loch Lomond Shores**, a gateway visitor attraction situated at Balloch. Within Drumkinnon Tower are viewing galleries and shops as well as two informative shows and a street theatre troupe. Here you can journey with a young otter through some of the myths and legends of the loch or watch and listen as the scenery becomes the backdrop to the story behind the song.

② The trail goes through the wood and passes into the ruined 19th-century farm steading of **Wester Sallochy** which the Forestry Commission has now cleared of trees. Several buildings can be seen and its worth spending some time investigating these old ruins and trying to imagine life in those times. When you have finished, circle the buildings to the left and follow the well-worn trail until it ends at a T-junction beside a waymarker post. Turn right on to the forest road here.

③ Follow the forest road for about ½ mile (800m) to reach a gate just before the junction with the main road. Cross the gate, then cross the main road and turn right. Look carefully for a faint track running through the woods to your left.

④ Follow the faint track back towards the loch (if you miss the track then enter the wood at any point and head west towards the

loch). When the track intersects with a well-surfaced footpath turn right. You are now on the **West Highland Way**. Follow the waymarkers, keeping on the main path and ignoring any subsidiary tracks branching off it.

⑤ Follow the path uphill through a rocky section and then, as it levels off, through a wood. There is some boggy ground here but strategically placed duckboards make the going easier. Eventually the trail passes through the **Sallochy Woods** car park returning you to the start.

WHAT TO LOOK FOR ⓘ
Large **oak trees** remain from when these woods were used to provide a constant supply of timber. They were under a coppice system of management throughout the 18th and 19th centuries which divided the area into a series of sections or 'hags'. Each hag was felled every 24 years but the best 400 trees would be left another 24 years and eight of these were spared to go on growing.

WHERE TO EAT AND DRINK ⓘ
Try the **tea room** of the garden centre on the shores of the loch at Balmaha. Here you'll find friendly service, food that is hot, tasty and nourishing and some dreadfully fattening cakes. Alternatively eat in one of several cafés and restaurants at **Loch Lomond Shores** where, as well as superb views, you'll find everything from snacks to seafood.

FOR BIRDWATCHERS
Apart from the capercaillie, these woods harbour that other Scottish speciality, the crested tit, and you might even be lucky enough to encounter a wandering Scottish crossbill too. Wildfowl gather on Loch Lomond in good numbers outside the breeding season, with goldeneye and scaup being among the highlights.

A Windy Walk to St Abb's Head

A refreshing wildlife walk along the cliffs.

•DISTANCE•	4 miles (6.4km)
•MINIMUM TIME•	1hr 30min
•ASCENT / GRADIENT•	443ft (135m) ▲▲▲
•LEVEL OF DIFFICULTY•	🚶🚶 🚶🚶 🚶🚶
•PATHS•	Clear footpaths and established tracks
•LANDSCAPE•	Dramatic cliff tops and lonely lighthouse
•SUGGESTED MAP•	aqua3 OS Explorer 346 Berwick-upon-Tweed
•START / FINISH•	Grid reference: NT 913674
•DOG FRIENDLINESS•	They'll love the fresh air, but keep on lead by cliffs
•PARKING•	At visitor centre
•PUBLIC TOILETS•	At visitor centre
•CONTRIBUTOR•	Rebecca Ford

BACKGROUND TO THE WALK

St Abb's Head is one of those places that people forget to visit. You only ever seem to hear it mentioned on the shipping forecast – and its name is generally followed by a rather chilly outlook – along the lines of 'north easterly five, continuous light drizzle, poor'. In fact you could be forgiven for wondering if it even exists or is simply a mysterious expanse of sea – like Dogger, Fisher or German Bight.

But St Abb's Head does exist, as you'll find out on this lovely windswept walk which will rumple your hair and leave the salty tang of the sea lingering on your lips. The dramatic cliffs, along which you walk to reach the lonely lighthouse, form an ideal home for thousands of nesting seabirds as they provide superb protection from mammalian predators. Birds you might spot on this walk include guillemots, razorbills, kittiwakes, herring gulls, shags and fulmars – as well as a few puffins. Guillemots and razorbills are difficult to differentiate, as they're both black and white, and have an upright stance – rather like small, perky penguins. However, you should be able to spot the difference if you've got binoculars as razorbills have distinctive blunt beaks. Both birds belong to the auk family, the most famous member of which is probably the great auk, which went the way of the dodo and became extinct in 1844 – a victim of the contemporary passion for egg collecting.

Luckily no egg collector could scale these cliffs, which are precipitous and surrounded by treacherous seas. Do this walk in the nesting season (May to July) and you may well see young birds jumping off the high cliff ledge into the open sea below. Even though they can't yet fly, as their wings are little more than stubs, the baby birds are nevertheless excellent swimmers and have a better chance of survival in the water than in their nests – where they could fall prey to marauding gulls. Neither razorbills nor guillemots are particularly agile in the air, but they swim with the ease of seals, using their wings and feet to propel and steer their sleek little bodies as they fish beneath the waves.

While the steep cliffs are home to most of the seabirds round St Abb's Head, the low, flat rocks below are also used by wildlife, as they are the favoured nesting site of shags. These large black birds are almost indistinguishable from cormorants – except for the distinctive crest on their heads that gives them a quizzical appearance. They tend to fly low over the water, in contrast to the graceful fulmars that frequently soar along the cliff tops as you walk, hitching a ride on convenient currents of air.

Walk 49 Directions

① From the car park, take the path that runs past the information board and the play area. Walk past the **visitor centre**, then take the footpath on the left, parallel to the main road. At the end of the path turn left and go through a kissing gate – you'll immediately get great views of the sea.

② Follow the track, pass the sign to Starney Bay and continue, passing fields on your left-hand side. Your

FOR BIRDWATCHERS
These extensive cliffs support Scotland's most accessible mainland seabird colonies. In addition to those species that nest here in large numbers, gannets can be seen offshore, visitors from their colony on the Bass Rock in search of feeding grounds. St Abb's Head is also a migration hotspot for land birds in spring and autumn; bluethroat and wryneck are among the highlights.

track now winds around the edge of the bay – to your right is the little harbour at St Abbs. The track then winds around the cliff edge, past dramatic rock formations and eventually to some steps.

③ Walk down the steps, then follow the grassy track as it bears left, with a fence on the left. Go up a slope, over a stile and maintain direction on the obvious grassy track. The path soon veers away from the cliff edge, past high ground on the right, then runs up a short, steep slope to a crossing of tracks.

④ Maintain direction by taking the left-hand track which runs up a slope. You'll soon get great views of the **St Abb's Head lighthouse** ahead, dramatically situated on the cliff's edge. Continue to the lighthouse and walk in front of the lighthouse buildings and down to join a tarmac road.

⑤ Follow this road which takes you away from the cliff edge. Continue to an obvious bend, from where you get your first views of the

WHAT TO LOOK FOR
One of the plants that grows on the cliffs is **scurvy grass**. You can spot it by its heart-shaped leaves and white flowers. It's high in vitamin C and was used by early sailors as a cure for scurvy.

Mire Loch below. You now follow the path downhill to the right, to reach a cattle grid.

⑥ Turn left here to pick up the narrow track by the loch, with the wall on your right-hand side. It's pretty overgrown at the start so can be hard to find, but it soon becomes much more obvious. Walk beside the loch and continue until you reach a gate.

⑦ Turn right along the wide track and walk up to the road. Go left now and continue to cross a cattle grid. When you reach a bend in the road, follow the tarmac track as it bears left. You'll soon go through a gate, then pass some cottages before reaching the car park on the left.

WHERE TO EAT AND DRINK
The **St Abb's Head Coffee Shop** at the visitor centre is open from Easter to October and serves a great range of sandwiches and light meals. You can choose from things like crab sandwiches, courgette and broccoli soup, toasted sandwiches, huge toasted teacakes and freshly baked cakes and scones. In Coldingham, the **Anchor Inn** serves a good selection of bar meals.

Extending the Walk
You can add a different dimension to your walk in this area by visiting the priory ruins in Coldingham. From the **harbour** in St Abbs, head south along the coastal footpath towards **Coldingham Bay**. A lane will take you up into the village where you can visit the priory. Return to St Abbs by following the main road until you reach the **Creel Road** path on your right. This will take you down into the back of St Abbs, above the harbour.

Ariundle Oakwoods and the Elements of Chemistry

Through the shades of green Sunart to the hillside site of an old lead mine.

•DISTANCE•	7 miles (11.3km)
•MINIMUM TIME•	3hrs 45min
•ASCENT / GRADIENT•	950ft (290m) ▲▲▲
•LEVEL OF DIFFICULTY•	术术 术术 术术
•PATHS•	Good through woodland, sketchy on open hill, no stiles
•LANDSCAPE•	Ancient oakwood, open and remote hill ground
•SUGGESTED MAP•	aqua3 OS Explorer 391 Ardgour & Strontian
•START / FINISH•	Grid reference: NM 826633
•DOG FRIENDLINESS•	On leads in reserve (Scottish Natural Heritage may relax this; look for signs)
•PARKING•	Nature Reserve car park at Ariundle
•PUBLIC TOILETS•	Tourist information centre, Strontian
•CONTRIBUTOR•	Ronald Turnbull

BACKGROUND TO THE WALK

What does Strontian have in common with the hamlet of Ytterby in Sweden, with Paris (Lutetia) and Copenhagen (Hafnia), with the planet Uranus and the Sun (Helios)? Chemical elements – the fundamental materials of nature. Seventeen of them are named after places, including ytterbium, lutetium, hafnium, uranium, helium – and strontium.

Davy the Namer

A new mineral was discovered in the lead ores of Strontian in 1793, and named strontites. Sir Humphrey Davy visited the mines in 1808 and isolated the new element strontium. Davy is remembered as the inventor of the safety lamp for miners, but he also identified and named the elements calcium, magnesium and chlorine. Strontium (Sr) comes in at number 38 in the list of chemical elements. When heated its salts burn with a crimson flame, and it is used in making fireworks. The radioactive form strontium 90 does not occur in nature at Strontian or anywhere else, but is produced in nuclear explosions, including the Chernobyl reactor disaster. Because of its chemical similarity to calcium, strontium 90 is absorbed into the bones, where its radioactive breakdown damages the bone marrow.

The Older New York

The lead mines around Strontian, including the Bellsgrove mine reached on this walk, opened in the early 18th century. The villages around them came to be known as New York, after the York Building Company that built them. Some 60 tons of Strontian lead – one tenth of the year's output – went in 1753 to roof the new castle at Inveraray. As the more accessible veins were worked out, these remote mines became uneconomic and eventually closed in 1871. They have been reopened in a small way for the extraction of the mineral barytes. The element barium, a chemical relative of calcium and strontium, is used in drilling muds for the oil industry.

On its way to the lead mine and the waterfalls of Strontian Glen, the walk passes through the Ariundle National Nature Reserve. In the mountains, the native wild wood of Scotland was the Scots pine. Here on the warm, damp sea coast, the wild wood is of oak. The Ariundle oakwood owes its survival to human interference. The livestock and deer that destroyed Scotland's forest were kept out so that the oaks could be coppiced – harvested on a seven-year cycle. The timber went to the iron smelters of Bonawe on Loch Etive and the oak bark to the tanning industry.

The wild oakwood is being repaired, with the felling out of commercial spruce. Beneath the dense canopy, it is carpeted in moss that even climbs the trees, and rich in ferns and primitive plants called liverworts. While we expect the natural world to be green, it's not often quite so green as Ariundle.

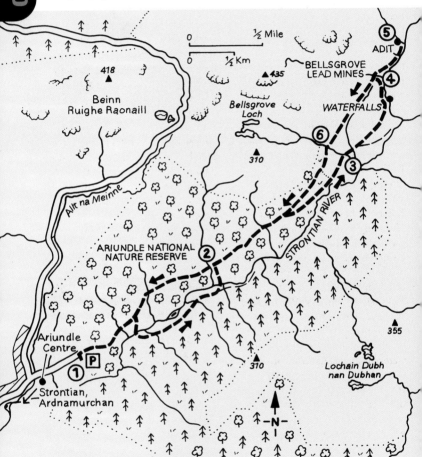

Walk 50 **Directions**

① From the car park, continue along the track into the oakwoods. After ½ mile (800m), a footpath turns off at a waymarker on the right. It crosses the **Strontian River** and heads upstream along it. After a pleasant ¾ mile (1.2km) it recrosses the river, following a duckboard section to rejoin the oakwood track.

② Turn right, away from the car park, to reach a high gate in a deer fence. The track immediately forks. Take the downward branch on the right to emerge into open grazings at river level. The track ends at a gate and stream.

WHERE TO EAT AND DRINK ⓘ

The **Ariundle Centre**, ½ mile (800m) from the start of the walk, has craft displays and a café with excellent home-made cakes. Dogs are welcome in the covered outdoor eating area.

---

③ Ford the stream on to a rough path. This crosses three more small streams, then forks. The lower, right-hand branch continues alongside the **Strontian River**, but the path, which is quite faint, slants up to the left to a solitary holly tree. Here it turns straight uphill for 50yds (46m), then bends right to slant up as before, passing 200yds (183m) below a bare rock knoll. The remains of wooden steps are in the path and a few cairns stand beside it. It steepens slightly to pass below a small crag with three different trees growing out of it – rowan, hazel and oak. With a large stream and waterfalls ahead, the path turns uphill and reaches the brink of the small gorge. Above the waterfalls, the slope eases and there is a footbridge down on the right which you don't cross; it acts as a useful landmark. Just above, the path reaches the broken dam wall of a former reservoir.

④ A green path runs across the slope just above. You can turn right on this, heading up beside the stream for about ¼ mile (400m). Here you will find a spoil heap; a heather bank marks the entrance to an adit – a mine tunnel running into the hill.

⑤ Return along the green path past Point ④, with the remains of the **Bellsgrove Lead Mines** above and below. The path improves into a track, following a stream down a small and slantwise side valley. As this stream turns down to the left, the track contours forward, to cross a wooded stream valley by a high footbridge above a waterfall.

⑥ A wide, smooth track continues ahead through a gate. After ½ mile (800m) it rejoins the outward route at the edge of the **nature reserve**. Follow the track back to the car park.

FOR BIRDWATCHERS

As you pass by streams and rivers, scan waterside boulders and you stand a good chance of seeing a dipper or grey wagtail, while the open moors are home to red grouse and golden plover. The ancient oak woodlands are home to resident common buzzards and great spotted woodpeckers, as well as migrant wood warblers and redstarts in spring and summer.

WHAT TO LOOK FOR ⓘ

You're unlikely to spot the shy **pine marten**, though there's a stuffed one behind the bar at the Nether Lochaber Hotel, on the mainland side of the Corran Ferry. The animal is like a large furry ferret and lives in the trees, eating baby squirrels. (Given the chance, pine martens actually prefer chocolate and jam.) A notice board on the nature trail points out, after you've passed it, that the duckboard section of the path is a place where they sometimes leave droppings – imagine a very small dog that's been on a diet of black treacle and you get the idea.

Walking in Safety

All these walks are suitable for any reasonably fit person, but less experienced walkers should try the easier walks first. Route finding is usually straightforward, but you will find that an Ordnance Survey map is a useful addition to the route maps and descriptions.

Risks

Although each walk here has been researched with a view to minimising the risks to the walkers who follow its route, no walk in the countryside can be considered to be completely free from risk. Walking in the outdoors will always require a degree of common sense and judgement to ensure that it is as safe as possible.

- Be particularly careful on cliff paths and in upland terrain, where the consequences of a slip can be very serious.

- Remember to check tidal conditions before walking on the seashore.

- Some sections of route are by, or cross, busy roads. Take care and remember traffic is a danger even on minor country lanes.

- Be careful around farmyard machinery and livestock, especially if you have children with you.

- Be aware of the consequences of changes in the weather and check the forecast before you set out. Carry spare clothing and a torch if you are walking in the winter months. Remember the weather can change very quickly at any time of the year, and in moorland and heathland areas, mist and fog can make route finding much harder. Don't set out in these conditions unless you are confident of your navigation skills in poor visibility. In summer remember to take account of the heat and sun; wear a hat and sunscreen and carry spare water.

- On walks away from centres of population you should carry a whistle and survival bag. If you do have an accident requiring the emergency services, make a note of your position as accurately as possible and dial 999.

Acknowledgements

Front cover: top Derwent Water, Lake District (AA/A Baker);
centre Swallows (AA/C Rose)
Back cover: top Crested Tit (AA/P Hayman); bottom Kestrel (AA/C Rose)